VERB TYPES AND TENSES

By Kevin Kirk

This book belongs to

Published by Indgenius Limited
61 Bridge Street, Kington, Herefordshire, HR5 3DJ, UK

This book forms part of the CORE English series, see the website for details: **www.englishbook.shop**

VERB TYPES AND TENSES
Written by Kevin Kirk
A CORE English Reference Book
1st Edition
First Published in 2019

ISBN 978-1-9160757-2-6

E&OE

www.englishbook.shop

ACKNOWLEDGEMENTS

This book is dedicated to the memory of Peter Kirk who died, aged 19, from diabetes related complications. Peter helped enormously in the initial stages of the creation of the CORE series. He compiled the phrasal verb and idiom lists and wrote most of the definitions and examples. He also provided many of the sample sentences in the noun and adjective books.

He is sorely missed.

This book is also dedicated to my wife, Thippanat. Without her it would never have been completed.

www.englishbook.shop

REWARD

Is the copy of the book you are holding genuine? Does it have a distinctive watermark on the reference pages? If not it might be an unauthorised copy. This book took 1,000s of hours to produce and just copying it is not only not fair but will force the price up for honest people like you. If you suspect this copy isn't real then please contact us via the website and you can be eligible for a reward.

www.englishbook.shop/copying

CONTENTS

CONTENTS

CONTENTS

CONTENTS

WHAT IS CORE ENGLISH?

CORE English is a methodology that was designed to make it easier for English language students to visualize how the language fits together in order to create grammatically correct sentences. In doing so it overturns, or modifies, a certain number of established grammatical 'rules'. It was based on over 7 years of research undertaken at Mahidol University in Thailand and was developed with the help and cooperation of over 2,000 students of varying abilities. The word CORE doesn't represent either an adjective or a noun, but, instead, it represents a verb as it basically cuts out certain sections of a sentence based on the central focus (i.e. the core) in order to study or modify them. In order to demonstrate the methodology in simple terms let us look at a particular sentence construct and how it is being taught at present:

In the afternoon a small number of the more health conscious students will be exercising.

Ok, so let's break that down into the constituent parts of speech:

In	Preposition
the	Definite article
afternoon	Noun
a	Indefinite article
small	Adjective
number	Noun
of	Preposition
the	Definite article
more	Comparative adjective
health	Noun
conscious	Adjective
students	Plural Noun
will	Modal Verb
be	Auxiliary verb
exercising	Present participle of the verb 'exercise'

Imagine being a learner and being confronted with that. When teaching a sentence construct like this you'd normally start with something simpler:

Today the students exercise.

This breaks down into:

Word	Type
Today	Adverb
the	Article/Determiner
students	Noun
exercise	Verb (Intransitive)

Now, what about if we used this same construct with the sentence on the previous page?

Word Cluster	Type
In the afternoon	Adverb
a small number of the	Article/Determiner
more health conscious students	Noun
will be exercising	Verb (Intransitive)

This, in essence, is what CORE is all about. It 'clumps' word clusters into types, which then become interchangeable. So, a beginner can start off with simple constructs and simply substitute more complex structures to add granularity and nuance to what they are trying to say. Ok, let's go through the construct above with some explanations:

Adverb: the above representation is a prepositional phrase, these are used to add granularity to where something appears in time or space. If we use the simple adverb, **today**, it gives us a broad idea of when something is taking place, but we may need to have more details, for example we may want to attend, so we use prepositional phrases. For example: **today** may be represented by the prepositional phrase **in the afternoon** and if we want to add even more granularity we simply add another prepositional phrase to indicate the start time, **from 2 p.m.** and we can also add an end time using another preposition phrase, **to 4 p.m.** So **today** and **in the afternoon from 2 p.m. to 4 p.m.** are interchangeable and can both be regarded as adverbs.

Article/Determiner: articles and determiners are usually regarded as special types of adjectives and, for the most part, are single use words that each have to be learned separately. In CORE they are treated as a special grammatical type and range from single words (like a, an, the, some or any) through to complex clusters consisting of various word types. Each cluster conveys a special meaning so the learner can move from the simple **the** (indicating a specific group) to **a small number of the** (indicating a particular subset of a specific group).

Noun: In most EFL classes we focus on the specific word(s) that attach a description (or label) to something, such that it can be recognised. In CORE this definition is broadened out using adjectives, so that nouns can be represented by noun phrases (as in the example above) or even adding verbs and adverbs so, what we consider to be noun clauses, are treated as simple nouns in terms of sentence construction. So the simple **'students'** could be replaced by the phrase, **'more health conscious students'** or a noun clause like **students who want to keep fit**. Grammar 'purists' would say that the noun clause example here is actually a noun (**students**) plus an adjective clause (**who want to keep fit**) but it is essentially interchangeable with a noun; so, in CORE it is regarded as a noun.

Verb: In CORE, verbs are regarded as single entities, so the simple bare infinitive verb **exercise** could be exchanged with a more complex structure, such as **will be exercising**, depending on the context. So all the learner has to do is to choose the action/state and then choose the tense/voice using the context.

To summarize, in CORE grammatical terms the following sentences have the same construct and elements within them and can be freely interchanged.

Today	the	students	exercise
⇕	⇕	⇕	⇕
In the afternoon from 2 p.m to 4 p.m	a small number of the	more health conscious students	will be exercising

TYPE CONSTRUCTS

Some of the grammatical constructs in the methodology are fairly rigid and unchanging, others are infinitely variable.

The main constructs are:

Adverbs (variable): single word adverbs basically consist of 5 basic types (plus adjective graduators and conjunctions), which can vary in terms of sentence position. These words are generally used to describe things like methods, probability or positions in time or space. These single words can be interchanged with the extremely variable (and flexible) prepositional phrases, which can add granularity to how, where or when something exists or has been done, how it was done and by how much.

Articles and Determiners (fixed): These constructs follow a predictable pattern, with the exception of some optional adjective graduators, so you can merely study the various definitions and choose the one that best suits your context using the **Articles and other determiners** reference book.

Nouns (variable): Nouns are primarily labels and have to be learned in order to recognise objects or entities (they are generally the first things we learn when we learn a language). Nouns are unique to every person and, in general, the larger the number of nouns the person knows the better their range of English. On the other hand we can thrive knowing only a subset of the total inventory of other types of words. In addition you must consider nouns that have been created from or using verbs (to describe actions or states rather than doing or experiencing them) ; such as, infinitives (usually to describe something that is intended to happen) and gerunds (usually describing something that has happened before or is ongoing). Noun clauses, which are mainly used to describe something where the corresponding noun is not known, are also regarded as, and interchangeable with, nouns.

Verbs (fixed): Verbs are the most structured and rigid grammatical constructs; therefore, in many ways they are the easiest to learn once the constructs are recognised. These constructs and contexts should be studied by looking at all of the choices and associated contextual meanings. This should focus on the way the verbs are used, not on the meaning of the individual verbs, as these can be looked up in a reference book once the use has been determined.

SUB-TYPE CONSTRUCTS

Introduction

Sub-types are used to vary the meaning inherent in the main type and sentence structures in order to add nuance or to create a better mental 'picture' in the mind of the listener or reader. They can also be used instead of the main constructs to add further detail to something that is already known (pronouns), to create a purely mental (abstract) image of what is being discussed (adjectives) or to get more information (questions).

Adjectives: These can be regarded as an adjunct to nouns. Nouns are how we understand our world, allowing us to visualise, or at least understand, whatever it is being talked about. In other words they refer to factual objects that we know to exist. Adjectives, on the other hand, tend to be based purely on imagination as we all relate to the things described by adjectives in a different way. A simple example is how a colour blind person imagines 'red' to how everyone else imagines it. Because they are imaginative constructs, adjectives, when used alone, describe abstract or relative concepts (like physical, mental or emotional states) and could almost be considered to be imaginative versions of nouns. They can also be used to clarify or add imaginative concepts to noun phrases and also act as standalone abstract references.

Conjunctions: Conjunctions are used to add words, phrases or complete sentences to the text, primarily in order to add clarity. In grammar they have a number of names associated with them (such as markers, conjunctions, conjunctive adverbs or subordinating conjunctives) but they all work in the same way, to add the 'glue' to bind grammatical structures together.

Pronouns: These are a subset of nouns. They are used in the same way as proper nouns or previously known nouns prefaced with **the**.

Infinitives: Infinitives are mainly used to indicate intent (usually after a verb and before a noun) or what something is used for. A present simple verb (such as am) is known as a **'bare infinitive'**.

Questions: These can be regarded as a subset of verbs as they generally involve verb/subject manipulation and a fairly rigid structure. The majority of question types involve subject/verb inversion (swapping) with so called 'wh' question words used to specify the type of answer that is expected.

MAKING VARIABLES

There are two constructs that are variable. The first are **adverbs**, which provide more details about the action or state, including the dimensional, characteristic or spatial qualities, that the objects and/or players in the sentence are witnessing, enacting or experiencing and the second are **nouns**, which describe the static objects or players in a sentence.

Adverbs: Adverbs add extra information to whatever action has taken place, is taking place or will take place. They are not required in the sentence but they answer questions about things like dates, methods, magnitudes or places. They can also add extra detail to adjectives and to join sentences of equal weight together. They can be in the form of single words, where they answer questions such as the manner in which something is done (how), the place where it was done (where), when it was done (when), the degree of what was done (how much) or the number of times it was done in a given time period (how often).

In order to provide answers to question that require complex answers they can take the form of prepositional phrases in order to answer questions above plus the cause of something, the content of something or the direction of travel. Prepositional phrases can generally be used to replace single word adverbs in order to add more detail - the prepositions reference in this series give examples for each of the prepositions in the corpus - and follow a particular pattern:

Preposition   Noun

The structure of the noun can vary, but the principle remains the same, where the preposition itself is used to announce that extra information is being given and then the noun provides the information. The noun can take a number of forms depending on the complexity of the information. For example, using the intransitive verb, go, we can use any of the following to add the information:

I went *there* (<u>simple adverb</u>)

I went *to* <u>the big park</u> (***prepositional*** phrase using a <u>noun phrase</u>)

I went *to* <u>that place we know</u> (using a <u>noun clause</u>)

Finally, if you need to associate an action, rather than a static image, to the extra detail you can add an adverb clause.

I went <u>where I always go</u> (<u>adverb clause</u>)

Nouns: Nouns are the heart of a sentence as they are the objects which do things, have things done to them or are used in order to create the result. They depend on the listener or reader having a mental image of what they are or represent and therefore they tend to be surrounded by extra detail, usually in the form of adjectives, in order to provide an exact picture. For example, we all know people and their mental image is recalled using their name. So, we can say something like 'I saw **Kate** today', where Kate is the noun. Which is fine if we only known one Kate, but what if we know more than one? In that case we can add an adjective to clarify what Kate we have in mind, usually by noting a particular attribute, so our sentence could read 'I saw blond **Kate** today', this is known as a noun phrase and can comprise of a number of preceding adjectives such as in the sentence 'I saw tall, beautiful, blond **Kate** today'.

Another way is to add another noun in order to create a compound noun, in which case our sentence could read 'I saw **Kate Jones** today'. If we don't know, or can't remember her name, then we can use a noun clause, so our previous sentence could be, 'I saw **that tall, beautiful blond girl I told you about** today'. Note that in each instance the sentence remains intact, 'I saw…today', with just the noun changing.

If we want to add further attributes to the noun, in the form of an active description, then we can add an adjective clause, so the sentence could now read 'I saw Kate **who I think is very beautiful** today'. Note that the adjective clause is added after the noun and in both instances the adjectives or adjective clauses are adding abstract characteristics to what is a static mental image.

In addition, rather than going through the tedium of describing Kate in every subsequent mention of her in the conversation, we can use a form of shorthand called a **pronoun.** So the sentence and follow on sentence could read 'I saw Kate today. **She** was going to the library'.

Finally, we often want to specify the noun and to do that we precede it with a determiner. In most grammar books determiners are counted as adjectives but in CORE they are treated as separate grammatical structures in order to make them interchangeable. In CORE, both adverbs and nouns are treated as single entities so they can be interchanged with other constructs of the same type whilst still retaining the correct grammatical structure.

CREATING SENTENCES

Using the constructs created on the previous pages we can now create a sentence. A simple sentence with a subject and object would look something like this:

Determiner	Noun	Verb	Determiner	Noun	(Adverb)
(null)	Fred	is eating	his	lunch	now

The null determiner in the first column is a place marker as we don't use a written determiner with a proper noun. The adverb is in parentheses as it is optional.

Determiner	Noun	Verb	Determiner	Noun	(Adverb)
The	dogs	drank	their	water	(null)

We can leave out elements without affecting the basic structure, for example with intransitive verbs with no objects but with a prepositional phrase to show how they did it (manner).

Determiner	Noun	Verb	Determiner	Noun	(Adverb)
Our	guests	left	(null)	(null)	in a car

We can see that the sentence can be defined in terms of a pattern and in order to help to visualise that pattern we can use colours, either by underlining each construct or by drawing directly onto a transparent overlay. The colours used in CORE are displayed on the back cover of this book and were chosen to provide the most memorable contrasts between the various constructs.

Sentences in CORE are built outwards starting with the chosen word/cluster type, then their associated support words. This is the exact opposite of the 'traditional' gap fill, where the correct type of word is inserted into a pre-written sentence. Although this looks to be harder it gives the benefit that contextually sensitive sentences can be produced, thus making it easier to 'think' the sentence.

The pattern used above is very simple and is a good starting point but more complex sentence structures can be built using more complex patterns and visualised using colours. The colours can be used to visualise the elements in a sub construct in order to see how complex constructs are formed.

PARSING SENTENCES

In order to help to visualise how a sentence is constructed in terms of its grammatical pattern we can go through it word by word using colours to highlight the words. Note, it is always a good idea to look for infinitives first (to + verb) and highlight them first (in orange) so you don't confuse them with prepositional phrases, then look for conjunctions in order to be able to recognise clauses. For example the following sentence:

The students who passed the exam are invited to receive a certificate from the Dean at 1 p.m.

This breaks down into:

The	determiner
students	plural noun
who	conjunction
passed	verb
the	determiner
exam	noun
are invited	verb
to receive	infinitive
a	determiner
certificate	noun
from	preposition
the	determiner
dean	noun
at	preposition
1	determiner
p.m.	noun

If we pull out the clause (prefaced with the conjunction) and the prepositional phrases we get:

The students...are invited to receive a certificate (main sentence)

who passed the exam (adjective clause)

from the dean (prepositional phrase)

If we look at the structure of the main sentence we see:

Determiner	Noun	Verb	Infinitive	Determiner	Noun
The	students	are invited	to receive	a	certificate

As we can see this is similar to our original sentence with the addition of an infinitive to express intent. The adjective clause that follows can be regarded as part of the noun as it helps to enhance it. The structure of the clause is similar to that of a sentence where the determiner and noun have been replaced by the pronoun, **who** (referring to the noun [students] that been mentioned earlier).

Conjunction	Verb	Determiner	Noun
who	passed	the	exam

This just leaves the prepositional phrases, which, as we discussed earlier, can be regarded as adverbs. The preposition phrases themselves have a fairly rigid structure usually consisting of:

Preposition	Determiner	Optional adjective(s)	Noun
from	the	(faculty)	dean
at	one		p.m.

Questions: Questions follow one of two main forms. The first is where the subject and verb the <u>auxiliary verb and subject are swapped</u> (aka inverted). These can be preceded by nothing, a pronoun, or an adjective or adverb form of a determiner. The main forms are:

<u>Are</u> <u>you</u> going?
Open question usually answered with yes or no

Who <u>are you</u> going to the cinema with?
Pronoun question word answered with a noun

Which movie <u>are you</u> going to see?
Determiner question word answered with a subset of noun choices

Where <u>are you</u> going to see the movie?
Adverb question word answered with a place or time

The other main question form is called a tag question and it usually consists of a sentence followed by (tagged on) a negative form of the verb, with the <u>verb and subject swapped</u>:

The students are seeing the dean, <u>aren't they</u>?

LEARNING WITH CORE

All too often English is taught as an academic subject hedged round with pages of rules that have to be memorised before a sentence can even begin to be constructed.

The philosophy behind CORE is to get straight down to writing grammatically correct sentences simply by plugging in pre-determined, constructs into an existing sentence structure. In other words it is learning by doing.

The way it works is to identify word/phrase clusters as being of a certain grammatical type - such as determiners, verbs, nouns or adverbs - and then substitute them for other words/phrases of the same type that express exactly what is wanting to be said. This was illustrated in the previous section.

In order for it to work the learner will need a fully explained corpus (essentially a detailed list) of sufficient grammatical types/words to cover the overwhelming number of variables. In other words a sufficient breadth to cover over 99% of all situations but not too many to be overwhelming and unwieldy to use. The final corpus used in the methodology uses just over 5,000 words. The biggest group are the nouns of almost 2,000 words, followed by over 1,200 verbs. These words were obtained by scraping documents of all types from around the world with a focus on spoken words (unlike most corpora, which are derived from purely written texts), slang words were then filtered out and, if thought to be important or used enough, included in separate sections (mainly in idiomatic speech in the idioms book). Then the words were categorised into their respective word types, if a word appeared in multiple word types, as many do, their frequency of use in that word type was studied to ascertain whether they warranted inclusion in that word type's corpus. If they were sufficiently commonly used in two or more categories comparisons in their use for each category were included, together with sample sentences, to highlight the differences.

After the sections had been created they were further categorised into use categories to make them easy to find and use. Examples of this are adverbs being categorised into manner, frequency etc or adjectives being categorised into descriptive types, such as positive and negative physical descriptors etc.

These were then written into separate books and their uses were described in detail. The resulting books should be regarded as reference or guidance books rather than 'learning' books. If they were to be categorised they'd fall somewhere between dictionaries and explanatory grammar books. Unlike grammar books they provide copious examples of the word/phrase use in different contexts and some contain exercises to practise self creation based on the principles using the learner's own writing. This allows the learner to create sentences within their own contexts rather than being constrained by those in the grammar book, which they may not understand and would find hard to use in their own work.

In order to parse the word/phrases out of existing sentences the use of colour is recommended. The books themselves are not coloured in order to keep the cost down but the recommended colours are shown on the back cover of this book: the individual book covers are also coloured to reflect the word types being explained. The colour palette was chosen on the basis that they are commonly available in the form of lost cost felt pens and/or coloured pencils and so the methodology can applied at very little cost. The individual colour assignments for each word type were chosen by a focus group who concentrated on the most recognisable resultant patterns once the individual words/phrases had been coloured. This allows the learner to see the grammatical structure of the sentence, particularly common problem types such as prepositions and determiners/articles. Using this method tracing paper can be used to 'lift the word types' from existing sentences by placing it over sentences and then colouring in the words. The resultant pattern can be used to create new grammatically correct sentences without being encumbered by the previous words in the sentence. In this way learners will see that certain sentence structures can be used to express particular grammatical forms (such as statements, questions, travel etc.)

Whilst researching the methodology inherent in CORE particular attention was paid to specific areas of difficulty that students were having in learning how to use English. These specific areas were then studied and simplified by restructuring them. One example of this is how verb tenses are approached; where, instead of saying that continuous/progressive tense consists of a verb plus auxiliary verb it would, instead, consist of a state verb and an adjective.

So 'I am running' is now **I** (pronoun) **am** (state verb stating what follows describes my physical state) **running** (the adjective that describes my physical state). This method simplifies the tense structure as the learner only needs to remember the tense structure of the state verb (a challenge in itself given the various forms of 'be') and then simply append a suitable adjective - with the choice based on the context so the same structure would apply to I am **running**, I am **hot** and I am **tired**, using a present participle, a simple state adjective or a past participle respectively - subsequently guiding the students to use adjectives based on present participles of verbs to talk about ongoing states is far easier than trying to parse tenses. Incidentally, tenses are covered in both the 'conventional' way and using the CORE methodology in the verb books so as not to confuse people who have already grasped the current principles and who merely want to see the nuances of how particular verb tenses are used and what they are used for.

Similarly with determiners, they now contain determiner phrases as well as individual words and they also include words that would 'normally' be regarded as, say, pronouns as determiners. Ask yourself this: if you are a learner you are told a pronoun is used <u>instead</u> of a noun and then you are told to put a 'possessive' pronoun in front of another noun would you be confused? It is far less confusing to regard the possessive pronoun as a determiner - which can be substituted by another determiner if required - than to run though a sort of mental boolean truth table of if A precedes X then it is B. The structure remains the same it is just the nomenclature that is changing.

Another area of difference between current English grammatical text books is in pronunciation. Pronunciation is the key to confidence and it is an important component in the books. It is based on the International Phonetic Alphabet (IPA) and uses the phonemes inherent in 'received' English (previously known as BBC English). This is not because of some sort of cultural imperialism but simply because if the students learn to pronounce all of the received English phonemes correctly then they are more easily understood. Moreover, there are 44 phonemes in received English, which allow more precise enunciation than the 38 in US English (when the early Americans left England they forgot to take most of the diphthongs with them).

Some changes were made in further simplifying the pronunciation of certain words, particularly verb participles, to make them easier to say and understand and an alternate alphabet is proposed. The dedicated pronunciation book covers this important topic in detail; moreover, each book in the CORE reference series features pronunciation for each word/phrase and a common pronunciation exercise. This exercise was carefully designed to include as many of the mouth shape (consonants), tongue position (vowels) and tongue transition (diphthongs) conjunctions as possible so as to provide a good introduction to the spoken language for beginners. It can also be used as a public speaking warm up exercise. Every book contains a short story, in the form of a fairy story, to whimsically introduce learners to the various words types.

Regarding the reference books themselves, each one focuses on the use of a particular word type and covers it in great detail, including copious examples of the word/phrase being used in different circumstances. They also cover such things as the origins of words, differences in pronunciation and spelling between UK and US pronunciation, comparisons of the same word when used in other forms and specific details applicable to that word type (such as collocations used to create phrasal verbs in the verb tables and whether nouns are countable, uncountable or both and whether they are used as verbs). Each word type book has a 'word/phrase/type finder' in place of a conventional index (the table of contents for each book is very comprehensive) so the learner/user can quickly find the right word/phrase/construct to suit their exact requirements. Finally, they also contain information and graphics to assist teachers in the classroom as well as being useful as reference books for individual learners or writers of all types who need to use the language.

In addition there are three books that underpin the reference books and contain an overall view of the language (Glossary), areas where learners make mistakes and a writing book that puts all of the methodology together in a simplified form. Finally, there is a website dedicated to the methodology, which contains discussion, exercises and answers, plus a range of useful tools. It can be found at:

www.englishbook.shop

ABOUT THIS BOOK

Verbs are the workhorses in every language. They describe actions or states, link two subjects together, describe both possibilities and when the action has or is likely to take place. They also have the most structured form of any phrasal form in English.

This book was designed as a reference book that shows you exactly how to use each type of verb in your work. Not only does it provide you with information about the different verb forms but it also all of the commonly used examples together with definitions and numerous sample sentences in order to show you exactly how to use them.

It covers the following topics:

- **State verbs**: this covers all of the commonly used verbs of this type together with sample sentences and descriptions.
- **Linking verbs**: this covers all of the commonly used verbs of this type to bring subjects together, with sample sentences to see how they work plus the description of each verb and how to recognise them.
- **Sense verbs**: these verbs describe how we interact with the world. It covers the commonly used verbs that use our senses (both in the concrete and abstract forms) plus examples and full descriptions.
- **Modal verbs**: these vital verbs are covered in depth, together with what they are used for and examples of their use. It also covers the semi-modals - verb forms that act like modals. Finally it covers how modals are used with perfect tense and used to describe how the past is effecting the present.
- **Transitive versus Intransitive verbs**: Shows how they're used, together with copious examples.
- **Passive versus active tenses**: how and why they are used and what they are used for.
- **Subject/verb agreement**: Describes how to choose the correct tense together with examples.
- **Tense formation**: this section covers what every tense is used for with examples of each use, their structure, how they are used with both intransitive and intransitive verbs, examples of every 'person' (including in the negative and question forms) with prepositional phrases and noun objects examples. This section covers every tense, both in the active and in the passive voice.

CORE BOOK SERIES

The CORE reference books currently include:

Writing in English: This book provides a step by step approach to how the various words and word clusters covered in the rest of the reference books are used in practise. It ranges from the formation of simple sentences, incrementally adding phrases and clauses in order to create compound and complex sentence structures. It also provides guidance about paragraph writing and leads on to essay and speech writing and structures. At the end of the book there is the CORE basic corpus, arranged by word type, in order for the learner to be able to recognise and change the words in the samples in order to create their own grammar constructs and a master contents for all of the books. It can also be used as pocket guide to writing with or without the rest of the CORE reference materials and would provide a handy guide to learners involved in formal English classes.

Adjectives: This book covers all aspects of adjective use such as placement, creation of comparatives and superlatives, noun substitution and clauses. It also categorizes common adjectives into useful categories in order for the user to choose the ideal adjective to suit their required meaning. There are also an adjective table, featuring all of the recommended adjectives in alphabetical order, together with sample sentences. These sentences have spaces underneath to allow the various word types to be colour coded according to CORE recommendations and/or add user sentences. There are no definitions under the adjectives in the main text are they are regarded as subjective (imaginary), but they are featured in the adjective selector.

Adverbs: This book covers adverbs in depth including such things as: adverb types, adverb placement, comparisons, and clauses. It also lists all of the recommended adverbs together with their meaning, their types, what prepositional phrase could be used to replace them and examples of their use. There is also a comprehensive adverb selector.

Common Mistakes and Pitfalls: This book covers commonly mistaken words and phrases and covers homophones, homonyms, commonly mistaken word comparisons, misspelled words and misused words. Contractions and abbreviations are also commonly misused and so they too appear in this book.

Articles and Determiners: Determiners and their subset, articles, are commonly misused and misunderstood. In fairness, for non-native speakers they are very difficult to use, with the, in particular, being commonly misused or omitted. This book looks at over 400 common noun types and subjects and studies the 'rules' on how **the** is used and the exceptions to these 'rules'. It also covers other types of determiners, including determiner phrases, that are usually referred to as pronouns or adjectives. There is also a determiner selector. It is a reference book for every non native English writer.

Changing (And Making) Words: This book is mainly about where certain types of words come from and how to convert words to other types of words using prefixes and suffixes, plus a section on the roots of many English words derived from languages like Greek and Latin. It also covers French, Latin, Scandinavian, Anglo Saxon, Greek and other source words and phrases that are commonly found in English today together with both their current meanings and their original meanings. It is ideal for creating new brand or product names.

Idioms: The use of English language idioms is a sign of a good understanding of the language; moreover, they are very commonly used and so a comprehensive reference is required to 'translate' them. This book contains over 4,000 of the most commonly used idioms together with their meanings and sample sentences illustrating their use in different contexts.

Key Verbs: This book covers the most commonly used verbs, which are found in over 80% of every day conversations and writing, and should be the first ones learned and thoroughly understood. To assist in this each verb is covered in depth listing each of its meanings, together with sample sentences. In addition there are examples of how the verb is used as or with a prepositional phrase, as an infinitive, with and in clauses, as a gerund, as a phrasal verb, in the passive voice, in its subjunctive form, in its adverb form, in its noun form and in its adjective form. Additionally, its past and present participles and the simple past are covered, with their respective pronunciation, together with whether it is used as a transitive, an intransitive verb or both. Finally its use in every tense for every person, both in the active and, if applicable (e.g. it is transitive), passive voice. The book also contains exercise sheets for every verb so it can be used in a classroom setting or for self study together with the website.

Nouns: This reference book takes a comprehensive look at the use of nouns using a carefully selected corpus that will cover over 99% of general English needs. It covers all of the different types of nouns including countable and uncountable nouns, recognising and creating nouns from other word types, gender specific nouns, compound nouns, portmanteau words, irregular nouns, common collective nouns, noun phrases and noun clauses. In addition it contains sections on nouns grouped by type, for example those use in specific circumstances and a list of recommended nouns together with their pronunciation, whether they are countable, uncountable or both and whether they are concrete, abstract or both. This section contains 1,892 recommended nouns together with sample sentences and definitions, comprised of 973 countable nouns, 239 uncountable nouns, 654 nouns that are both countable and uncountable, 20 nouns that are only ever used in the plural form and 6 that are only ever used in the singular form.

Numbers, Days, Dates and Time: This book takes a comprehensive look at the use of numbers, days, dates and times in English. It covers such topics as how they are presented (numerically or in words), formats, uses and origins. The book also supplies various numerically based tables covering such things as computer numbering, ASCII, including extended ASCII, and other computer based codes as well as tables showing numbers such as UNICODEs and colour codes. There are also various graphics for use in the classroom.

Question forms and other Miscellany: This book takes an in depth look at question formation and their uses in clauses. It also contains a glossary of English terms plus a wealth of other information such as how to recognise and use conditionals, conjunctions, interjections, euphemisms, anagrams, differences between UK and US English, British understatement, oxymorons, palindromes, metaphors and similes. There is also a section listing all the countries of the world together with links to further information.

Phrasal Verbs: phrasal verbs are commonly used in English and usually have a different meaning to the bare infinitive version of the verb. They may also have more than one meaning depending on the context. This book lists 1,500 of the most commonly used phrasal verbs together with over 2,000 meanings and sample sentences. It also has a phrasal verb selector so you can find exactly the right verb.

Prepositions: Prepositions are the most commonly misunderstood words in English, yet they are very commonly used and thus vital to learn. This book takes a comprehensive look at prepositions; covering such topics as what prepositions are, how prepositions can be used as a more comprehensive form of adverb, using prepositions in speech, answering questions using prepositions, categories of prepositions, the origins of common prepositions and the use of prepositions with pronouns, nouns and noun phrases. There is also a preposition selector to help you to find exactly the right preposition to suit your needs. The use of prepositional phrases as adjectives, using prepositions with noun clauses, how prepositions were derived and a list of the most commonly used compound prepositions including meanings and sample sentences are also included. Finally, it takes a comprehensive look at the currently most used prepositions together with their various meanings (they invariably have more than one meaning) and how they are used in various contexts, together with numerous sample sentences.

The alternative to nouns - Pronouns, Infinitives and Gerunds: This book explores the various types of word forms that can be used instead of nouns to change nouns from passive objects to active (verb based) objects and to avoid repetition. The infinitives section covers the formation and use of infinitives to express such things as intent and their use as adjectives and adverbs. It also covers collocations with adjectives and certain verbs and contains a comprehensive list of the most commonly used infinitives, together with sample sentences. There is also a guide to how infinitives and gerunds, based on the same verbs, are used in various contexts.

The gerunds and present participle section highlights the uses of gerunds and how gerunds and present participles, although appearing to be the same, are different. It includes a section containing the 1,000 most commonly used gerunds and present participles showing how they are used in sample sentences. Finally the pronouns section covers the various types of pronouns and there is a pronoun reference section containing all of the commonly used pronouns in use together with a definition of their use, their pronunciation, their type (indefinite, subject, object etc.) and what verb tense needs to be used with them. There are also numerous sample sentences and each pronoun has a comprehensive comment section outlining all aspects of the use of the pronoun in English.

Pronunciation: Correct pronunciation is the key to confidence when learning English and this book focuses on English pronunciation in its many forms. It takes a very comprehensive look at the subject including subjects such as: a short history of English (why we speak like we do), the IPA symbol charts, creating consonant sounds, consonant/letter tables, creating vowel sounds, mouth parts involved in speech, creating diphthong sounds, vowel letter pronunciations, pronouncing the 'ed' ending of verbs and past participles and vowel and diphthong phoneme uses. The uses section covers how individual phonemes are used in various combinations in English words, each of which is accompanied by a large number of sample words, so the learner can practise the sounds of that phoneme within the word structures, and exceptions (and samples) are included to show where and when the pronunciation differs. In addition there is a British English practise section highlighting why British English sounds different to US English. There is also a long vowel and diphthong association section, including US and UK pronunciation differences, a section on stressing words and syllables and also a comprehensive section on the use of silent letters - including the most common words containing silent letters and the history showing why the letters are silent as well as the exceptions. Finally there is a complete set of IPA flashcards, which can be copied and used in the classroom. The pronunciation audio files are available on the website. (www.englishbook.shop).

Punctuation and Use of Capitals: This book provides a comprehensive guide to the use of both punctuation and capital letters. Each punctuation symbol is covered in depth together with numerous example sentences. Obsolete and rarely used symbols are also covered as well as intellectual property symbols and planetary and astrological symbols. It also covers the use of codes, such as bar codes, QR codes and Morse code. Greek symbols are also covered, both in their upper and lower case forms, together with their various uses in English. There is even a free font that accompanies this book that includes all of the special characters, including things like Braille, Runes and religious symbols (including the Bahai 9 pointed star) amongst others; with a guide on how to easily insert them into your writing. The use of capital letters sections covers such things as using capitals in sentences and in formal correspondence. There is also a section on the use of certain types of punctuation under special circumstances or to add stress.

THE WORLD OF THOUGHT

A Fairy Story

Welcome to the world of thought. In our world we have an aristocracy, called the pronouns, led by the first person, 'I'. I almost always leads the parade (called sentences in your world) it is present in, unless questions are being asked, in which case I is preceded by its personal bodyguard verb 'am'. 'You' is I's closest confidant and is the second person in the kingdom. Other, less senior, pronouns like he, she and it are the third persons. If I belongs to a group it gets a special status and name, 'we' (the royal we), signifying the group includes the first person.

If I isn't in the group then it is automatically relegated to third position and given the name they. I also has a body double called 'me', as do he (him), she (her), we (us) and they (them) when they are loitering, unprotected, at the end of the parade. 'I' doesn't want 'you' to get above itself so 'you' isn't given a body double and has to share a bodyguard, are, with we and they. The other pronouns have to share a bodyguard, is, with the nouns.

The middle class are called the nouns and their only job is to describe something. The nouns are always trying to achieve a higher status by being recognised by the determiners. The grandest of these is 'the', who, together with its lesser acolytes, 'a' and 'an', have the name 'the articles'. It is considered a great honour for 'the' to walk in front of a noun in the parade marking them out as being special. If 'the' doesn't consider the noun to be worthy (for example 'the' likes rivers and forests but not lakes or cities) then the nouns can hire the lesser (impoverished) pronouns to walk in front of them in the parade as their determiners or even appear instead of them (but I and You are far too grand to do this), giving the impression that they are well known enough not to appear in person. When 'the' makes 'a' or 'an' stand in front of a noun it announces to the world that the noun isn't special at all but is just one of many (the is a bit of a coward and would never do that to a group of nouns – although 'the' will use 'some' to walk in front of uncountable numbers of positive nouns or 'any' in front of ones 'the' considers to be negative or questionable). 'The', being a civil servant, likes to count things - so it often gets numerical pronouns to walk in front of plurals. 'The' is very jealous of 'I' and has a yearning to lead the parade. In written parades 'the' is more popular but in spoken parades 'I' is the still the most popular.

Having very little to do, nouns are constantly striving to appear less boring, so they hire make-up artists, beauticians, hairdressers and PR executives, called adjectives, to walk in front of them. Adjectives boast that they can flatter any noun ('we can make any girl beautiful' it says on their website). Nouns can also hire adjectives to make their rival nouns look ugly or stupid.

The world has a police force, called the prepositions, who walk in front of the nouns telling the subjects where to go, what to do and when to do it. As in your world, the little ones are the most authoritarian; always ordering the kingdom's subjects to go <u>to</u> a place, <u>by</u> a certain time, <u>on</u> a certain day and be either <u>in</u> or <u>out</u> of a place <u>at</u> a specific time. On the other hand the big, fat desk sergeants, like around and about, are far more easy-going.

Then there are the working class; the verbs. They are simple folk and like to do a job once and then relax but they are often made to do repetitive jobs. They have their children (called the 'ings'), who are continually running round and their old people (the 'eds') who like to reminisce about things they did in the past. The problem, for these simple verbs, is that the ings and eds keep getting kidnapped and put to work by the nouns and adjectives. The nouns even give the children a middle class name, 'gerund', whereas the adjectives prefer the name participles ('It reminds us of flowers. Beautiful, exciting, fragrant, tropical, colourful, sensual flowers,' said an adjective spokesword). The gerunds are made to dress up as nouns and talk about the work their parents do, so the nouns can pretend they are workers too. Adjectives make the ings stand in line with other adjectives and categorize nouns or to rush round, while being guarded by an auxiliary, continually doing things for the pronouns or nouns. Meanwhile, the eds are made to go on chat shows and talk about the feelings that the nouns or pronouns are experiencing or their great achievements.

The simple verbs tried to get help from the other tenses but the perfects, being young professionals with no ings of their own, had no time to talk about it. Time is not important to them; it's results that count. And the perfect continuous, being teenagers (they still have a bit of 'ing' in them, even though they try to look grown up by adding 'ed' to their name), spend all their time complaining about how long they've been forced to do something for. The simples did approach the newspaper reporters, the passives, who wrote tear-jerking editorials then went off for long, expensive lunches. They are called passives because they don't do any work themselves they just report and comment on things that other people do and spread gossip (usually without saying who did it, in order to avoid being sued).

CORE English Reference Book

Intransitive verbs cannot become reporters as they aren't considered acquisitive enough to require any objects (reporters must acquire objects to write about) and usually summon a police word to walk after them to protect them if an object tries to follow them around (the other words mock them by calling them 'phrasal verbs' to indicate they have lost their true meaning).

The politicians, called the adverbs, were also approached but they were more interested in pretending they had a hand in whatever work it was that the verb was doing. You can tell who they are because they always appear in the parades wherever they like (they have even been known to walk in front of I) in order to show themselves off. So when a poor verb has done the work the adverb pops up to say how, when, where or how difficult it was to do, thus trying to claim the credit. Many of them were adjectives before becoming politicians and give themselves the title 'ly' (like 'mp' in your world) after their name to show they no longer have to indulge in grubby trade nor do they have to deal with nouns, except to grade them and they only do that through an adjective. Other, older ones, like today and tomorrow, can trace their ancestors right back to the prepositional phrases, so they don't need 'ly' to gain the respect they need to lead, or trail, a parade.

The lawyers, the conjunctions, weren't a lot of help either. All they do is add clauses (to make things clearer they say) and spend most of their time giving long winded explanations of nouns or appearing for nouns or adverbs. Some politicians are still involved in their previous legal practises and make a very good living as conjunctive adverbs bringing two equal parties together, but they are always shielded from other, lesser, words by ';' and ','. All of the simple tenses suffer, even the 'irregulars', so named because they are regarded as hippies as they like to do things differently, who tried to give their 'eds' different names to try and disguise them but with limited success.

As far as the punctuation are concerned, nobody ever listens to them, in fact everyone stops talking when they show up. They are there to clear up after the parade has passed and they are often misused. However, the periods are armed with a sickle when questions are being asked, or a club when strong statements are being made, in order to act as a rear-guard. Commas simply clean up part way through long parades, especially when fussy, non-defining conjunctions are involved, and inverted commas just highlight what people say. Not many people seem to know what the colon family does, although there are whispers that the weird looking cousin, semi colon, (the one with a permanent leer) is a sort of super comma and people generally change the subject when the perpetually shocked colon appears.

CORE English Reference Book

The pronouns and favoured nouns have their own special category of armed verbs working for them, called the auxiliaries, who had been recruited many years ago, mainly from Germany, and who protect the pronouns by walking just behind them in a parade or standing in front of them when potentially hostile questions are being asked.

They also have their sages, the modals, who, despite changing the entire mood of a parade, are considered useful because they can predict the future or provide reasons why past events are effecting the present.

There are also palace functionaries, called the state verbs, whose job is to provide a link to the adjectives and nouns (a pronoun is far too grand to have direct contact with a mere tradesman like an adjective or a noun) to let people know how or what the pronoun, or favoured noun, is feeling or what they are thinking.

The paralegals, named linking verbs, can be hired by nouns to directly compare themselves with other nouns or even pronouns in order to flatter themselves. Linking verbs, being professionals, rarely exhibit any emotion and tend to just provide a connection between two or more things.

Anyway, I'd love to tell you more about our world but here comes the parade.

Oh dear, 'the' isn't going to like that; being made into a mere object by honouring a simple, unadorned noun like that.

I am leading the parade.

CORE English Reference Book

PRONUNCIATION EXERCISES

Read each sentence aloud slowly, pronouncing each word as carefully and properly as you can. Do not pronounce the numbers at the start of each sentence. The underlined parts of the words are the phonemes that correspond to the IPA symbols in the right hand column.

Vowels and Diphthongs	Symbol
1) Each team's dream keeps them lean and mean	iː
2) They mainly aimed to play the same game	eɪ
3) Fred said the dreaded red bed's ahead	e
4) Pretty women hit lit nymph's lips in Italy	ɪ
5) I dried my right eye by Guy's night light	aɪ
6) Oh no Joe don't throw goats at my beau	əʊ
7) After class a sergeant marked father's parked car	ɑː
8) Awed audience applause bored Claudia	ɔː
9) Pulling wool could be good for a full woman	ʊ
10) Whose gruesome true new ewe oozes wooziness	uː
11) Gert hurt germs burning her wormy shirt	ɜː
12) Demure juries sure cure pure manure	ʊə
13) Joyce's moist boys enjoyed choice oysters	ɔɪ
14) Mere seers near here fear tiered deer	ɪə
15) Town clowns frown at brown cows on couches	aʊ
16) A happy cat sat on a plaited mat in Nat's flat	æ
17) Where prayerful bears stare at a mare's hair	eə
18) Father's aggrieved about Italian national cinema	ə
19) Bud loves running up other muddy ruts	ʌ
20) Lots of hot grog rots soggy pods	ɒ

Pronunciation Practise Continued

Consonants	Symbol
1) Peter Piper Picked a Peck of Pickled Pepper	p
2) Brian's big brother breeds bad brown bears	b
3) Ted tried Tony's tame tricks ten times on Tuesday	t
4) Dan's dusty dogs desperately drink despite dining	d
5) Churlish Churches each churn cheddar cheese	tʃ
6) Julie conjures up large jamborees during June	dʒ
7) Kevin Kirk's caterwauling creates constant confusion	k
8) Good Greeks give big garish gliders guiltily	g
9) Four foul fellows flooded Feltesham fen	f
10) Violet's vicarious vanity veered vividly vertical	v
11) Beth thinks things thoroughly through	θ
12) The tethered brother bothered their mother	ð
13) Citizen Sam saw several ceremonial cedars	s
14) Lazy zoos freeze hazardous zebras	z
15) Shirley sure shines at shearing garish shipshape sheep	ʃ
16) Azure treasures leisurely pleasures	ʒ
17) Many men move momentous mountains	m
18) Nine nurses knew newts gnawed nuts	n
19) A phalanx of singers wearing rings sang songs	ŋ
20) Hubert's hut happily hosted Harry's harmonium	h
21) Lucy likes looking at lovely lilac lace	l
22) Restless Rhinos roam Rwanda's roomy forests	r
23) Wally wore warm Wellingtons when it was wet	w
24) Yes, Vignette's yellow onion yields yards of yogurt	j
*Note: Rwanda is pronounced /ruˈæn.də/	

VERB OVERVIEW

Verbs are the words in a sentence that indicate an action, a state of being (physical, mental or emotional), the possession/experience of something(s), to link two or more things, to sense something or, when used with another verb, to express necessity or possibility.

For **Example:**

I <u>ran</u> quickly.   (*I took part in the **action** of moving fast*).
I <u>am</u> now hot. (*This is my physical **state***).
I <u>had</u> a shower. *(I **experienced** a shower).*
The shower <u>was</u> cool. *(Shower **linked to** cool).*
I <u>saw</u> a spider in my shower. (*I **sensed** something*).
I <u>might</u> run again later. *(Describe a **possibility**).*

<u>Action verbs</u> are the most commonly used verbs in English as most of our experiences are about what we do, rather than what state we are in or what we own.

<u>State verbs</u> (aka stative or abstract verbs) talk about the physical, mental or emotional states that we experience.

<u>Possessive verbs</u> talk about what we own or hold. These possessions can be in the form of something physical (like a car or a computer), an attribute (like intelligence or a good memory) or an experience.

<u>Linking verbs</u> show the relationship between things. They do not represent an action and convey no emotion, they merely state what the speaker considers to be a fact.

<u>Sense verbs</u> describe how we physically interact with the rest of the world. In particular they describe how we interpret our immediate surroundings.

<u>Modal Verbs</u> are used to add ability, advice, compulsion, habits, orders, permission, possibility, probability and regret to verb constructs. They are also used to indicate future actions or states (as English does not have a future tense) and, together with present perfect, to talk about events in the past that are effecting the present.

All of these verb types are covered in their own sections later in the book.

VERB FORMS

Verbs can take three forms in English: the base form (for example **eat** – also known as the bare infinitive form), the conjugated form (for example **eaten, ate** or **eating**) or the infinitive form (example **to eat**). With the exception of '**be**' and the modal verbs, all English verbs have two conjugations in the simple present (for **Example: sleep** and **sleeps**) and only one in the simple past (**slept**). The verb '**be**' differs in having three conjugations in the simple present (**am, are, is**) and two in the simple past (**was, were**). Modal verbs are not conjugated but semi-modal verbs are (i.e. **have to** *or* **has to**).

__Participles of verbs__ (examples: **walked** – past participle and **walking** – present participle) are used to create verb phrases. Present participles are used in continuous tenses (**I am walking**) and past participles are used in perfect tenses (**I have walked**) and in the passive voice (**The dog was walked**). Past participles are formed, in the majority of verbs, by appending the letters '**ed**' to the base verb. These are called **regular verbs**. If the past participle cannot be formed by merely appending '**ed**' but are, instead, a completely different construct, they are called **irregular verbs**. These are covered in depth in the reference section later in the book.

__Auxiliary verbs__ are generally used to form tenses in English. They have two characteristics: They can be inverted to form questions (**She is going** – statement form | **Is she going?** – question form) and they can be followed by the word '**not**' to indicate a negative statement (**I am not going**) or a question (**Is he not coming?**). The auxiliary verbs in English are: **be, have, do, dare** and the modal verbs.

__Transitive verbs__ [T] need a direct object, usually in the form of a noun, noun phrase, noun clause or a pronoun. They are generally action verbs that describe an action that can be seen to be done. In English the prefix '**trans**' means across, so a transitive verb acts as a bridge between the subject and the object.

__Intransitive verb__ [I] although they are generally action verbs, they do not need an object and can be used to form very simple sentences.

Note that some verbs can be used as transitive and intransitive verbs.

Example: I went (intransitive) *or* **I went home** (transitive).

TENSES AND VOICES

<u>**Voices**</u> are divided into active voice - where the action or state is performed by, or related directly to, the subject - and passive voice - where the action or state is imposed upon, or directed to, the subject, or is carried out by someone who is unknown or unnamed.

<u>**Verb Tenses**</u> are covered in more detail later on in the book. However, as a brief introduction the main differences are explained here by taking a quick look at how we would use various (present) tense forms, with the verb **work**. For this we will create four different sentences using the four tense forms:

I **work** with Mark.   Present simple.
I **am working** with Mark.   Present continuous
I **have worked** with Mark.   Present perfect
I **have been working** with Mark.   Present perfect continuous

<u>**Present Simple**</u>: is being used here to say that I work with Mark every day. It doesn't mean we are continuously working together (we have to sleep sometimes), but he is someone who works in my office.

<u>**Present Continuous**</u>: is being used to say that for the duration of something the person who I am with is Mark. This could, for example, be a certain project - **I am working with Mark on verbs** - or during a certain time - **I am working with Mark in this class.**

<u>**Present Perfect**</u>: is being used to say that Mark is one of the people that I have had the experience of working with. He could be one of many or it may have just been him.

<u>**Present perfect continuous**</u>: is being used to say how long I have worked with Mark, with an emphasis on the duration. I would normally use the words **for** – to indicate the length of time – or **since** – to indicate the point in time in which we started working together.

As they are all present tense it means that the fact that I am at work with Mark is true at the moment. If my period of working with Mark has finished then I'd use the past tense, as shown on the next page.

Verb Types

TENSES AND VOICES

I **worked** with Mark.	**Past simple.**
I **was working** with Mark.	**Past continuous**
I **had worked** with Mark.	**Past perfect**
I **had been working** with Mark	**Past perfect continuous**

All of the circumstances for using the tenses are still valid (such as the fact that Mark and I worked together), but it is not happening any more. I'd use the simple to state the fact that he and I worked together as colleagues at one point in time and the continuous to state that we had worked on something together but are no longer doing so. The perfect would be used to say that I had the experience of working with Mark at some point in the past and the perfect continuous to say that we had worked together for a certain period of time but I am no longer working with him.

Finally, I would use the future tense to say that I will work with Mark, again using the tense types to be more specific about the circumstances, but here I am anticipating something that is likely to happen in the future, but hasn't happened yet. The tenses are:

I **will work** with Mark.	**Future simple.**
I **will be working** with Mark.	**Future continuous**
I **will have worked** with Mark.	**Future perfect**
I **will have been working** with Mark	**Future perfect continuous**

In this tense, the simple future just says that I am certain I will work with him or to make the offer of working with him. The continuous states that I am going to be doing something with him for a certain length of time at some point. The perfect states that I will have had the experience of working with him in the past and it is still true and the perfect continuous says that I will have worked with him for a certain length of time, at some time in the future (for **Example:** I will have been working with Mark **for a year in December** – where '**for a year**' states the time period and '**in December**' states at what point that time period is being measured to).

ABBREVIATIONS

Many of the verb structures you will use in the following sections have abbreviations associated with them. These are not normally used in written speech – with the exception of fiction or transcripts – but they are used in spoken speech. The following table lists most common abbreviations and their pronunciation.

Structure	Abbr.	Examples	Pronunciation
am	'm	I'm	aɪm
are	're	You're, we're, they're	jɔːr, wɪər, ðeə
are not	aren't	You aren't	juː ɑːnt
is	's	He's, she's, it's	hiːz, ʃiːz, ɪts *
is not	isn't	She isn't	ʃiː ˈɪz.ənt
was not	wasn't	It wasn't	ɪt ˈwɒz.ənt
were not	weren't	They weren't	ðeɪ wɜːnt
will**	'll	I'll, you'll, he'll, she'll, it'll, we'll, they'll	aɪl, juːl, hiːl, ʃiːl, ˈɪt.əl, wiːl, ðeɪl
shall**	'll	I'll, you'll, he'll, she'll, it'll, we'll, they'll	aɪl, juːl, hiːl, ʃiːl, ˈɪt.əl, wiːl, ðeɪl
will not	won't	It won't	ɪt wəunt
have	've	You've, we've, they've	juːv, ˈwiːv, ðeɪv
have not	haven't	We haven't	wiː ˈhæv.ənt
had	'd	I'd, you'd, he'd, she'd, it'd, we'd, they'd	aɪd, juːd, hiːd, ʃiːd, ˈɪt.əd, wiːd, ðeɪd
had not	hadn't	They hadn't	ðeɪ ˈhæd.ənt
has	's	He's, she's, it's	hiːz, ʃiːz, ɪts *
has not	hasn't	She hasn't	ʃiː ˈhæz.ənt

* Note 1: these two abbreviations are pronounced in the same way so you must learn to recognise what is meant from the context or from the following verb structure.

** Note 2: these two abbreviations are both pronounced in the same way and used in the same way (shall is mainly applicable to the first person; whereas, will is applicable to all persons).

VERBS OF POSSESSION

We attach great importance to the things we own, whether they are concrete, such as physical possessions or abstract, like memories. The most commonly used possessive verbs are shown below:

Verb	Meaning	Sample Sentence
Acquire	Add to your possessions	I **acquired** a new coat.
Amass	To accumulate possessions	He **amassed** a great fortune.
Belong	Used to state where the ownership lies	The coat **belongs** to me.
Bring	Carry something here	I **brought** a chocolate cake.
Buy	Get by paying money	I **bought** a computer.
Clutch	Hold firmly	She **clutched** her purse tightly.
Collect	To perform action to get	He **collects** stamps.
Control	Exercise authority usually by having possession	She **controls** the household budget.
Detain	Hold for a defined period	He was **detained** by the police.
Get	Have something given or sold to you	I **got** a coffee from my students.
Grab	To take suddenly	I **grabbed** my keys off the table.
Have	Absolute ownership	I **have** a black dog.
Hold	To both have and keep safe	The suspect was **held** in a cell.
Liberate	Possess by armed force	The army **liberated** the town.
Lift	Pick up & take without consent	He **lifted** it and put it in his pocket.
Obtain	Get possession of	I **obtained** a new telephone.
Own	List possession(s)	I **own** a phone and a computer.
Possess	List attribute(s)	I **possess** a dreadful memory.
Purloin	Another word for steal	He **purloined** a pen off my desk
Retain	To possess in a secure way	I **retained** the key for the house.
Seize	To take possession by legal (by law) force	His assets were **seized** by the court.
Steal	Take stealthily & without consent	I **stole** a biscuit from her desk.
Take	To remove without consent	I **took** the wrong umbrella.
Withhold	Keep control of	The bank **withheld** the deeds to his house.

SENSE VERBS

Our interface with the world

Our senses are how we interact with the world and so the verbs used to describe our senses are fundamental to our existence. However, they often have meanings that go beyond the original purpose and can be used, usually in an abstract sense, as both state verbs and dynamic verbs.

On the following seven pages the verbs most associated with the five main senses are covered together with other verbs that share an association.

In addition to the physical senses we also have the ability to 'know' about something without knowing why and the main verb we use to describe it is the verb **'sense'** (She **sensed** she was being followed).

This regular verb was originally derived from the noun sense, meaning to be inwardly conscious of something without being able to explain why or how. This noun came, in turn, from the old Latin word **'sensus'** meaning perception, understanding, feeling and knowing.

The words **senseless** (originally meaning without sensation but now generally known to mean stupid or thoughtless – It was a **senseless** piece of vandalism) and **nonsense** (silly or stupid idea – What is this **nonsense** I hear about you leaving us?) were derived from it.

This word is more commonly used in the noun form where it has three main meanings: ability to use one of the body's senses (see, smell, touch, taste or hear) to understand or react to something (My dog has a very good **sense** of smell), to exercise good judgement (I hope you have the **sense** to realize that what you've done is wrong) or to possess a meaning (This essay makes absolutely no **sense**).

Notes

TOUCH

The verb, 'feel', was originally a noun and was documented in the early 13th century where it had the meanings of sensation or understanding. It started to be used as a verb, meaning the action of sensing something in a tactile way, around 200 years later. It was derived from the old English word '*felan*' meaning to touch or perceive using a sense that has no specific organ assigned to that sense.

In the early 20th century the phrasal verb '**feel up**', meaning to sexually molest, started to be used. The noun (gerund) '**feeling**', describing an emotion, is what someone feels inside themselves (I have a **feeling** this will all go wrong).

A number of words have been derived from it, or are closely related to it, such as **feeler** (proposal advanced to gauge reaction), **resent** (feel badly about), **grasp** (reach for or feel around), **tentacle** (from the Latin, '*tentatus*' meaning to feel), **consent** (from the French '*consentir*' meaning to feel together), **rue** (feel regret) and **tempt** (meaning to feel out or try to influence). As a verb it is mainly used, nowadays, to mean **touch** (Can you **feel** the lump on my head), opine (I **felt** I had to tell her that I didn't love her any more) and experience (I **feel** really bad today, I think I have the flu). Other 'touch' verbs are shown below:

Verb	Meaning	Example
Caress	Touch lightly in a loving way	She **caressed** her new baby.
Embrace	Hold tightly in a loving way (i.e. family/lovers)	The lovers **embraced** each other lovingly.
Feel	Perceive by physical sensation	He **felt** for the light switch.
Fondle	Handle in a sexually suggestive way.	Watch how he **fondles** the melons in the market.
Hug	Hold tightly to express pleasure	Friends often **hug** on meeting.
Kiss	Touching lips together	He **kisses** his wife every day.
Massage	Manually manipulate	Can you **massage** my back?
Pat	Tap lightly	He **patted** his dog.
Pet	Stroke lightly (Mainly US)	She **petted** her cat.
Rub	Press firmly with movement	He **rubbed** his sore muscles.
Squeeze	Grasp while applying pressure	He **squeezed** my hand.
Stroke	Rub lightly in one direction.	He **stroked** her hair.
Touch	Perceive using tactile feedback	He **touched** it and it felt hot.

TASTE

The verb, 'taste', was originally derived from the Latin word *tastare*, meaning to feel or touch. From this word the old French word *taster* meaning the sense by which a flavour can be discerned was derived and from that the anglicised word, *taste*, was created.

In the late 1600s, it was first used as a noun to signify aesthetic appreciation (She has a good **taste** in clothes) and to indicate flavour (This soup has a nice **taste**). A number of words have since been derived from it, such as the adjectives **tasteful** (having or showing an appreciation of aesthetic qualities – it was a **tasteful** display of her art), **tasteless** (meaning insipid or likely to upset someone – He told a **tasteless** joke at the funeral), **distasteful** (meaning distressing – Politicians seeking political points out of disasters is regarded as **distasteful** by most people) or **tasty** (meaning a nice flavour – I think Miso soup is very **tasty**).

In its verb form it is regular and can be used as a stative verb meaning that something has a certain (agreeable – positive *or* disagreeable - negative) flavour, expressed using an adjective: This food **tastes** delicious (agreeable) *or* I think this coffee **tastes** bitter (disagreeable).

It can also be used as a dynamic (action) verb meaning to briefly experience something (Once you have **tasted** the high life you never want to be poor again) or to sense flavour using the mouth (The chef **tasted** the sauce to check if it was too salty).

The sense of taste is probably the most subjective of all the senses (in other words its classification is based on personal perceptions); as such, it is often used in an abstract sense meaning to do something for a brief time. Other 'taste' verbs are shown below:

Verb	Meaning	Example
Discern	Recognise a taste	I **discerned** pepper in the dish.
Relish	Enjoy a pleasant taste	I **relished** the Chicken Tikka.
Sample	To taste a small amount	The food judge **sampled** all the food.
Savour	Take as long as possible to enjoy a taste.	I **savoured** the taste of the Tom Yung Khung.
Taste	Sense with the tongue	It **tasted** very salty to me.
Test	Try to perceive flavour	I **tested** the soup for saltiness.

SMELL

The exact origins of the verb, 'smell', are unknown, however it is very closely related to the late 12th century old English noun 'smell', meaning an odour (neutral), stench (negative) or aroma (generally positive). It is also closely related to the negative irregular verb stink.

In the UK, the verb smell is irregular (both the past simple and the past participle is **smelt** pronounced /smelt/); whereas, in US English it is regular (past simple and past participle is **smelled** pronounced /smel.d/).

As well as meaning 'detect an odour' (That **smells** nice), it can also mean that someone is aware of a (usually bad) situation and is often expressed in a metaphorical way. Bad smells are excellent metaphors as we protect ourselves against ingesting something poisonous by detecting the odour and so we are conditioned to avoid bad smells.

For example, it can be used to say that someone has a sense that something is not right (I **smell** a scam) or is not correct (I think this deal **smells** fishy), in this latter context it is also used as a noun (I don't like the **smell** of this).

Other 'smell' verbs are shown below:

Verb	Meaning	Example
Breath (in)	Take in an odour deliberately (phrasal verb).	She **breathed in** the tang of the sea breeze.
Inhale	Breath deeply in order to analyse the smell.	I **inhaled** deeply in order to determine the smell.
Perfume	Create a nice smell	She **perfumed** her wrists with her new eau de toilette.
Scent	Detect faint odour	My dog **scented** the fox.
Smell	To detect an odour with the nose.	I can **smell** freshly baked bread.
Sniff	To hold up to the nose to catch an odour.	She **sniffed** the clothes to see if they smelled fresh.
Stink	To create a bad odour.	He **stank** the house out with his cigarette.
Whiff	To get a brief smell of something. (UK slang)	Once she **whiffed** his smelly feet she quickly left the room.

HEAR

The verb, 'hear', was derived from the early German word *hauzjan* (later becoming *horen*), meaning to listen, obey, follow or judge. The adverb *here* originally shared the same spelling, but the two words diverged in the late 12th century. A number of words have been derived from this verb such as; **hearken** (listen to), **hark** (to make someone listen), **hearsay** (rumour – possibly derived from **I hear**d her/him **say**), **hearer** (person who hears), **hearing** (perception by ear *or* the proceedings in court, committee or tribunal) and **overhear** (hear something that wasn't intended to be heard).

In current usage it is used to become conscious of a sound (I **hear** sleigh-bells, it must be Santa Claus), to be told news (Have you **heard** about what happened to her?) and to listen attentively (I **heard** some disturbing news on the radio today). It is also used as a phrasal verb, **hear from**, meaning making contact with someone (You'll be **hearing from** my lawyer *or* don't do anything until you **hear from** me).

It is commonly used in idioms: **Hear me out** (Let me explain), **I can't hear myself think** (It is too noisy), **Long time, no hear** (We haven't spoken for a long time), **I hear you** (Mainly US: I understand), you **could hear a pin drop** (It is very quiet), **have you heard** (Give someone some gossip), **that's not what I heard** (That isn't my understanding of it), **I never heard a dicky bird** (nobody told me - UK), **the last we'll hear of it** (The subject will never come up again) and I will **never hear the last of it** (I will be constantly reminded of something).

Verb	Meaning	Example
Catch	To hear and understand.	I'm sorry I **didn't quite catch** that. (Note, the negative sense).
Eavesdrop	Listen without the speaker's knowledge	I **eavesdropped** on her conversation with Julie.
Hark	To order someone to listen (archaic)	If you **hark** carefully you'll hear the nightingales singing.
Hear	Perceive sound	Did you **hear** the program on the radio?
Heed	Pay close attention to what is being said	You need to **heed** what he says, he really knows this subject.
Listen	Hear with intention and close attention	**Listen** carefully, I'll only say this once.
Overhear	To unintentionally hear a conversation	I **overheard** them saying they were going to rob the bank.

SIGHT

This is the most precious of all the senses and the one which is commonly used in an abstract sense; for example, when the speaker is asking the listener(s) to 'see' something in their mind. In fact, every sentence needs the reader/listener to 'see' what is being discussed.

The irregular verb most associated with this sense, 'see', was derived from the old English verb *seon* meaning to look, behold, observe, perceive, understand, experience, inspect or visit. It is also the root of the words 'say', 'seed', 'seek', seem', 'seer' 'seethe' 'foresee' and 'follow' (as in sequel). Some etymologists believe that the original meaning was 'follow with the eyes'. It is a very commonly used verb with numerous meanings:

Meaning	Sample Sentence	Example Tense
Meet	I **saw** my girlfriend last night.	Past simple
Understand	I **see** the problem.	Present simple
Consider	I **couldn't see** myself as a soldier.	Present + modal
Go with	I **saw** my girlfriend home after our date.	Past simple
Try to discover	I **will see** if I can find a solution.	Future simple
Make certain	I **will be seeing** that it is done.	Continuous
Check	I will go **to see** for myself.	Infinitive

It can be used as both a state verb (I **saw** her running) and an action (dynamic) verb (I **see** my wife at lunchtime every day).

It is often used as an intransitive verb, where it signifies understanding. For example if someone is explaining a problem or a situation, then the listener can signify that they understand – but don't necessarily agree - by saying "I **see.**" For example, Student: My dog ate my homework. Teacher: **I see.** Do you really expect me to believe that?

Finally, it is used in a number of phrasal verbs. For example:

Verb	Meaning
See about	To arrange *or* to consider something *or* to speak to somebody to get something done
See into	Accompany someone into an office
See off	Chase something away *or* go to say goodbye to someone
See out	Accompany a guest out *or* live beyond a certain point
See through	Continue to the end *or* notice that someone is lying
See to	Deal with or fix something

SIGHT

Verbs used for vision: The following table lists all of the commonly used sight verbs, plus their meanings and pronunciations. Some of them refer to seeing in the abstract sense (seeing with the inner eye).

Behold bɪˈhəʊld	To observe with wonderment. I **beheld** all the great things she had done in her life.
Browse braʊz	To casually look with little interest I idly **browsed** through a magazine.
Discern dɪˈsɜːn	To see something that is not clear I **could** only just **discern** him in the dark.
Envision ɪnˈvɪʒən	To see something in the mind I **envision** that there will be a disaster.
Examine ɪgˈzæm.ɪn	To discover by looking carefully The Police **examined** the crime scene.
Eye aɪ	Look warily at someone or something He **eyed** up his opponent before the match.
Foresee fəˈsi	To see beforehand *or* to anticipate I **foresee** problems with this plan.
Gawk gɔːk	Look on with amazement or stupidly He **gawked** as she beat the guy at arm wrestling.
Gaze geɪz	To look for a long time I **gazed** at my wife across the room.
Glance glɑːnts	To take a quick, short look I **glanced** across at her but she didn't see me.
Hallucinate həˈluː.sɪ.neɪt	To see things that don't exist He **hallucinated** after taking the drug.
Look lʊk	To deliberately seek out with the eyes I **looked** for a place to park my car.
Monitor ˈmɒn.ɪ.tər	To watch and check over time We **monitored** the situation carefully.
Notice ˈnəʊ.tɪs	To see something for the first time I **noticed** she had come home early.

SIGHT

Observe əbˈzɜːv	To watch carefully (formal) They **observed** the enemy's movements.
Peer pɪər	To look intently in order to find She **peered** through her curtains at her neighbours.
Perceive pəˈsiːv	To see something obvious I **perceived** an error in the document.
Peruse pəˈruːz	To look through carefully I **perused** the document carefully.
Picture ˈpɪk.tʃər	To see in the mind I **pictured** my perfect house in my mind.
Review rɪˈvjuː	To look again I **reviewed** the plan looking for flaws.
Scrutinize ˈskruː.tɪ.naɪz	To look at something extremely carefully The lawyer **scrutinized** the document.
See siː	To briefly catch sight of something without intent I just **saw** a beautiful butterfly.
Spot spɒt	To finally see something after looking hard for it I finally **spotted** her in the crowd.
Spy spaɪ	To look in a secretive or furtive manner Her neighbour **is spying** on her.
Squint skwɪnt	Partly close eyes in order to see more clearly He had to **squint** because the sun was so strong.
Study ˈstʌd.i	To examine academically (i.e. in an expert way) The expert **studied** the old painting.
View vjuː	To decide by looking carefully or see for the 1st time He **viewed** the car he wanted to buy.
Visualise ˈvɪʒ.u.əl.aɪz	To see an ideal situation in the mind using imagination She **visualised** a world where poverty was banished.
Watch wɒtʃ	To look for a long period at continuous action **Did** you **watch** the game on TV?
Witness ˈwɪt.nəs	To see something as it happens I **witnessed** a bad traffic accident.

AUXILIARY VERBS

Auxiliary verbs (also known as helping verbs) are regarded as a class of verb that marks tense, aspect, mood or voice. There are only a few auxiliary verbs in English but they add a substantial amount of power to the language and a lot of confusion to learners. The most commonly used auxiliary verbs are **be, have** and **do** which are all irregular verbs that are used in forming verb tenses as well as being main verbs in their own right. **Be** is used as a main verb to indicate the state the subject is in - physical, mental or emotional - **have** is used to indicate possession and **do** is used to indicate undertaking an unspecified action or to add emphasis.

They can also be used in subject | verb inversion (where the **subject** changes places with the <u>verb</u>) to form questions.

Statements: **She** <u>is</u> happy. (using **be** – note the object is an adjective)
Question: <u>Is</u> **she** happy?
Statement: **She** <u>has</u> arrived. (using have)
Question: <u>Has</u> **she** arrived?
Statement: **You** <u>did</u> eat (using do – in this case to add emphasis)
Question: <u>Did</u> **you** eat?

Note that only auxiliary verbs can be used to form questions in this way. When using other verbs in inverted questions use '**do**' to form the question. The main verb, **go**, will no longer describe the tense and will revert to its simple present (base) form. The auxiliary verb, **do**, will now describe the tense.

Statement: **She** <u>went</u> to the market (with past tense of verb **go**).
Question: *Did* **she** <u>go</u> to the market?

Note, you can also use **do** instead of the correct verb when you are not sure of what action verb to use.

Example: I **do** the crossword every day.

The correct, but unknown, verbs are **complete** or **attempt.**

Other auxiliary verbs that can be used in this way are the modal verbs (but not the semi-modals), which are described in detail in the modal verb section later in this book.

LINKING VERBS

Linking verbs are used to connect two things and can be divided into two types: firstly, there are verbs that describe a current state such as: **appear, be, feel, remain, seem,** and **sound.** Secondly, there are verbs that indicate a result of some kind: **become, get, go, grow** and **turn.** Their object is often an adjective, rather than a noun. The most common linking verbs are:

Verb	Meaning	Sample Sentence
appear	Seems to be	He **appears** hungry.
be	State of being	I **am** hungry.
become	Start to be	I suddenly **became** tired.
feel	Experience something	I **feel** tired.
get	Obtain *or* be awarded	I **got** fired.
go	To travel or move somewhere	I **go** fishing on Thursdays.
grow	Get larger or more pronounced	I **grew** ever more angry.
keep	To stay in a physical state	I **kept** quiet.
lie	To lay horizontally	He **lies** on the bed.
look	Appears to be	That lion **looks** angry.
prove	Confirm as fact	His work **proved** my theory.
remain	Stay in same place or condition	He **remained** calm.
resemble	To look like	He **resembles** my father.
run	Tend to be	Tempers **run** hot in this town.
seem	To give the effect of being	He **seems** relaxed.
smell	Detect something using a nose	The food **smelled** delicious.
sound	How something seems to be	The idea **sounds** crazy.
stay	Continue in a state or place	They **stayed** quiet.
taste	Detect flavour using a tongue	The food **tasted** odd.
turn	Change to another state	The meat **turned** rancid.

In order to tell if a verb is a linking or an action verb substitute the verb with **be** derivatives (such as **am, are** or **is),** or use **and,** then check if the sentence still makes sense, if so then it's a linking verb:

He **appears** *hot* – substituted: *he* **is** *hot works;* so, it is a linking verb
He **appears** *when he likes* – substituted: *he* **is** *when he likes* does not work; therefore, it is an action verb.
She **looks** *lost* – substituted: *she* **is** *lost* works; so, it is a linking verb.
She **looks** *for a book* – substituted version: *she* **is** *for a book* does not work; so, it is an action verb.

STATE VERBS

State (or stative) verbs are used to describe things such as physical feelings or positions, senses, possessions, emotions, thoughts or mental processes. They are known as abstract verbs as they cannot usually be seen to be performed or are static (not moving). As opposed to most action, or dynamic, verbs they may, in fact usually do, take an adjective as the object rather than a noun.

State verbs do not generally take the passive voice. However, that rule is sometimes ignored (He **is loved** by all his followers *or* the play **was disliked** by the audience) particularly in newspaper reports.

They can be in the present, past, or future tense; however, because they generally describe static conditions, they are generally regarded as not being able to progress through time; so, it used to be the 'rule' that they could not be used in the continuous tense. This 'rule' is commonly being ignored these days (for **Example:** "I'm loving it"), especially where they are used to describe a temporary action that has already started.

In order to recognise state verbs you need to know that they generally fall into one of the categories below:

Examples	Category and Description
Emotions	
dislike, hate, love	To try to describe something that has no definition
Mental feelings	
concern, realise, sit	To describe your rational thought processes
Physical feelings	
ache, feel, itch	To describe a feeling in your body
Possessions	
have, own, want	To describe things you have or want to have
Senses	
hear, see, smell	To describe what your senses are telling you
Thoughts	
believe, regret, think	To describe emotional or logical thought processes
Knowledge	
consider, know, understand	To describe knowing about something

STATE VERBS

The following list covers all of the commonly used state verbs. Note: the definitions are in the context of state verbs and are not always applicable to the same verbs used as action verbs.

Verb	Definition	Example
Ache	To suffer mild pain	I **ache** all over my body.
Agree	To have same opinion	I **agree** that something needs to be done.
Appear	To seem	It **appears** to be broken.
Astonish	To surprise someone	I'm **astonished** that he came top in the exam.
Be	Describe state	I **am** hot, she **is** cold, they **are** wet
Believe	Think something is true or should be true	I **believe** in equal justice for all.
Belong	Be in the right place	He **belongs** in prison.
Concern	Cause anxiety	I'm **concerned** about your poor attendance.
Consider	Think about	I **consider** the matter is closed.
Consist	Be made of	Her account **consists** of a lot of speculation.
Contain	Hold something inside	The kids couldn't **contain** their excitement.
Contemplate	Consider future action	I **contemplated** giving to charity.
Decide	Make a choice	I **decided** to eat noodles.
Deny	To declare untruth	He **denied** ever meeting her.
Depend	Rely on	I **depend** on her to help me.
Deserve	Have earned something	He thinks he **deserves** respect for his PHD.
Disagree	Not have same opinion	I **disagreed** with everything he said.
Dislike	Not enjoy or approve	I **dislike** opera *or* I **dislike** what you do
Doubt	Feeling of uncertainty	I **doubt** if he'll be here on time; he never is.
Fear	Think negatively	I **fear** we will never know the truth.
Feel	Have an opinion	I **feel** we should consider his idea.
Fit	Be suitable	He will **fit** well into our department.

STATE VERBS

Verb	Definition	Example
Forget	Stop thinking	He tried to **forget** all about her as it hurt too much.
Hate	Strongly dislike	I **hate** his new car *or* I really **hate** him
Have	Possess	I **have** a new car.
Hear	Learn by hearing	I **hear** what you are saying (= I know)
Imagine	Think about in abstract	I **imagine** she'll want a new dress now.
Impress	Cause admiration	He **impressed** her with his intelligence.
Include	Make part of something	We must **include** her in the discussion.
Itch	Have skin irritation	My leg **itches** because I have a rash.
Intend	To have an aim	I **intend** to finish this book soon.
Involve	Include others	Writing the test **involves** many people.
Know	Have knowledge of	I can't prove it but I **know** he is wrong.
Lack	Something missing	This essay **lacks** any sort of reasoning.
Lie	Deceive with falsehood	She **lies** about everything.
Like	Enjoy or approve of	I **like** reading spy novels.
Loathe	Strongly dislike	I **loathe** his selfishness.
Look	Appear or seem	My dress **looks** good or The report **looks** ok
Love	Feel strong affection	I **love** my wife very much.
Matter	Be important	It **matters** to me if we don't get a pay rise.
Mean	Intend	I **mean** to carry on despite the setbacks.
Measure	Discover exact size	The nurse will **measure** your blood pressure.
Mind	Oppose something	I don't **mind** if you eat the last piece.
Need	Have to have	I **need** a new car as mine is unreliable.
Owe	Need to repay	I **owe** money on my car loan.
Own	Belonging to someone	Who **owns** the white car in the car park?
Please	Make someone happy	The new recipe **pleased** her family.
Ponder	Think carefully	I often **ponder** the meaning of life.
Possess	Have something	He **possesses** a PHD in gardening.
Prefer	State a preference	I **prefer** coffee instead of tea.
Promise	Say with certainty	I **promise** I will tidy up my bedroom.

Verb Types

STATE VERBS

Verb	Definition	Example
Promise	Say with certainty	I **promise** I will tidy up my bedroom.
Realise[1]	Understand a situation	He **realised** the importance of studying.
Reason	Judge based on facts	I **reasoned** that she is not very bright.
Recognise[2]	Know something	I **recognised** you immediately.
Regret	Be sad about	I **regret** to say there were no survivors.
Remember	Recall from memory	I just **remembered** where I left my keys.
Remind	Make aware again	She **reminds** me to take my medicine.
Resemble	Perceived as being alike	She **resembles** her mother.
Satisfy	Provide relief	I hope you are **satisfied** with our plans.
Sit	Be pleased about	That decision doesn't **sit** well with me.
See	Understand	I **see** what you are trying to say.
Seem	Judged to be	It **seems** that I was wrong.
Smell	Detect odour with nose	This meat **smells** bad.
Sound	Something that seems good	That **sounds** like a great idea.
Stand	Be in a state or situation	His debts **stand** at over $1,000,000.
Suppose	Think likely	I **suppose** I'll have to do it as you won't.
Surprise	Effect of unexpected	I'm **surprised** he bothered to come.
Surround	Be all around	She **surrounded** herself with mementoes.
Taste	Detect flavour	This food **tastes** delicious.
Think	Consider	I **think** that's a great idea.
Understand	Know meaning	I **understand** what you are telling me.
Want	Desire something	I **want** to visit Japan.
Weigh	Determine heaviness	Step on this and it will **weigh** you.
Wish	Express desire or regret	I **wish** I was rich *or* I **wish** I'd learned Thai
Wonder	Question yourself	I **wonder** if she likes me.

[1] The alternate spelling of this verb is realize.
[2] The alternate spelling of this verb is recognize

www.englishbook.shop

MODAL VERBS

Modal verbs are a subset of auxiliary verbs and are all used with other verbs to express ideas such as possibility, permission and intention. However, one of their most important uses is to express the future, because the English language does not have a future tense as such. They are also used to form questions and to add conditions to sentences using the perfect tense. Because of their versatility they are some of the most flexible and powerful words in English.

Before moving on to the modals it is first worth considering words that are not modals, but are used like modals. These are generally referred to as semi-modals. They are often prefaced with the relevant version of 'be' (I am... You are... He is...) or have/had/has and are commonly followed by the infinitive version of the verb. They are described below:

Semi-modal	Use to	Sample Sentence
(be) able to	Express having the capability of doing	He **was able to** fix the engine.
dare to	Express that a risk is being taken	He **dared to** challenge her story.
(be) going to	Express action taken after a lot of thought	I'm **going to** do a PHD.
(be) going to have to	Express that an action is being forced	He's **going to have to** resign.
had better	Express that it is an important action	You **had better** confess.
(have/has) got to	Express best course of action to take.	You **have got to** report this.
used to	Something that was true, but not now	I **used to** smoke a lot.
want to	Express desire for something	Now, I **want to** eat some chocolate.

The most commonly used modal verbs are shown in the table below; Note they are arranged in terms of their relative strengths from left to right (strongest is will: weakest is could):

Will	Have (to)	Must	Need (to)	Shall	Can
Ought (to)	Should	Would	May	Might	Could

The following pages provides the most common uses and sample sentences for each modal. The negative versions are in parentheses.

MODALS WITH PERFECT TENSE

Modals are used with present perfect tense verbs to describe actions in the past that effect the present (or the future).

Examples	Meaning
They **will** have left by now.	Definite assumption of completed action
She **has to** have sold the watch.	Logical conclusion
I **must** have left my mobile phone at work.	Only possible conclusion
You **need to** have got a degree in order to get this job.	State requirements
We **shall** have done the work before you get back.	1st person definite
I **can** have had an ice cream as I'd eaten all my vegetables.	Strong possibility
She **ought to** have thrown him out years ago.	Best course of action
I **should** have listened to my mother.	Regret at not doing something
I **would** have gone <u>but it was raining</u>.	<u>Reason</u> something was not done
I **may** have been a little hasty in my assessment.	50% possibility
I **might** have left if it hadn't been so interesting.	Vague possibility
I **could** have been famous if I'd stayed in my rock band.	3rd conditional (impossible)

Note: in the list of modal verbs **need to, ought to** and **have to** are listed as modals (and indeed are often used as modals, which is why they appear in the list) however they are not regarded as modals by many grammarians as they can take the 's' form for 3rd persons (She has to eat *or* He needs to eat) and the 'to' should belong to the following verb to make it an infinitive.

When using these particular modals, together with the present participle of the verb, put a 'be' between the modal and the verb (I **have to be** going. She **ought to be** arriving soon. I **need to be** there).

WILL (WON'T)

This modal tends to be used to indicate a definite action or an imperative.

It differs from 'going to' in that the modal verb 'will' is generally used to indicate a spontaneous decision to do something (**I will** have an ice cream), whereas going to indicates an action that will be undertaken. after a great deal of thought (I am going to visit my mother *or* I'm going to study for a PHD).

Use for	Sample sentences
Habitual behaviour	He **will** always be getting into trouble.
Insistence (note the word **will** is stressed in the sentence)	You **will** wash the dishes before you go out, young lady.
Making a decision	Ok, ok I **will** go with you tonight.
Carefully consider a decision with reluctance	Hmm, I **will** really have to think about that.
Making a promise	I **will** pick you up at eight.
Making a semi-formal request	**Will** you go to the movies with me this evening?
Making a threat	I **will** fail you if you don't start handing your work in on time.
Making deductions	The balance of payments deficit **will** lead to a fall in the pound.
Making personal predictions	This new program **will** save me hours of work.
Offering to do something	I **will** give you some help with that if you are stuck.
Reassuring someone	Don't worry things **will** get better soon.
Talking about the past with certainty	She **won't** have caught the train or she'd be here by now.
Talking about the present with certainty	Now, we **will** go for a walk.
Talking about the future with certainty	Next year **will** be our best year ever.

MUST (MUSTN'T)

This modal is most commonly used to express an obligation that the subject has placed upon themselves (I must go on a diet). It is <u>never</u> followed by an infinitive (I must ~~to~~ go shopping).

Note: the negative is pronounced /ˈmʌs.ənt/, where the 't' in the word 'must' is generally silent.

Use for	Sample sentences
Expressing that something is imperative when imposed on oneself.	I really **must** go on a diet as I gained nearly a kilo while I was on holiday.
The negative **mustn't** indicates a prohibition derived from law.	You **mustn't** smoke in here.
For expressing necessity	This book **must** be given back after use so others can use it.
Strong advice	You **must** study if you want to pass your exams.
Saying you <u>think</u> something is certain	It **must** be ten years since I saw you last.
Expressing obligation	I **must** call my wife and tell her I'll be late home.
Pressing for acceptance	You really **must** come to my party tonight.

Notes

HAVE TO (DON'T HAVE TO)

This modal is mostly used to express an obligation placed on the subject by someone else (**I have to** get to work by 9 am). It is used with a following infinitive form of the verb and it has to match the subject (have or has) or the tense (have/has or had). The negative version is prefaced by **do not**; however, this is commonly pronounced as **don't** in speech.

Use for	Sample sentences
Have to is used when someone else has imposed the imperative.	You **have to** finish these accounts as I am relying on them.
Don't have to indicates that there is not an obligation to do or not do something.	You **don't have to** come with me to the meeting if you don't want to.
Giving very strong advise based on knowledge (for example knowledge of relevant laws).	You **have to** keep your driving documents in your car.
Mild admonishment after someone else's actions.	You **don't have to** be like that, I was only doing my best.
To complain about being made to do something.	Do I **have to?**
To give strong advise based on experience.	You **have to** save every minute when you use this software as it is really unstable.
To state an obligation despite being against it.	You **don't have to** like it, your job is to obey.
To provide a better alternative when being forced to do something.	**Have to** renew your car insurance? Come to us and we'll save you money *or* If I **have to** wash the dishes can I at least listen to the radio?
Being strongly advised to pursue a course of action to prevent big problems later.	You **have to** go to see the doctor as that lump on your breast may be serious.

Notes

NEED TO (NEEDN'T)

This modal is commonly used to express something that the person has got no real choice about doing (I **need to** go to the toilet) or is being obligated to do. When it is used in the positive sense (**need to**) it uses a following infinitive form of the verb and it has to match the subject (need or needs) or the tense (need/needs or needed). The negative version is followed by a simple verb and doesn't depend on the subject or the tense – in other words it acts like a true modal verb.

Use for	Sample sentences
To express that you want something very much	**I need to** go and see that new movie.
Forced by physical circumstances to do something	**I need to** see the dentist about my toothache.
Forced obligation (based on what is expected by social convention).	She **needs to** visit her sick cousin in hospital.
Speaking about attending to urgent bodily needs.	**I need to** find a toilet urgently.
With the third person singular (only) we would use **needs to** rather than **need to**.	She really **needs to** have her hair done: it's a mess.
The negative form is always **needn't** for whatever person is being referred to.	You **needn't** take that tone of voice with me young lady.
To state that something didn't have to be done even if the rules said it should.	You **needn't** fill out the register now, we'll do it later when you've freshened up.

Notes

____

____

____

____

____

____

SHALL (SHALL NOT)

This modal is mostly used with first person (I shall… or We shall…). In US English, and in certain dialects in UK English, it is slowly going into disuse and is being replaced by 'will', which has the same abbreviation ('ll). There is an alternative (slang) version of shall not, shan't (ʃɑːnt), which is only used in speech and is mainly used when someone is emphatically refusing to do something (I shan't do it!).

Note, the modal '**should**' is regarded as the past form of shall.

Use for	Sample sentences
In the first person, singular or plural, indicates definite intention	I **shall** go shopping, if I have the time.
In other persons it shows an order or command.	You **shall** be taking the exam at midday.
Making offers	**Shall** I open the door for you?
Asking for suggestions	What **shall** I make for lunch?
An obligation to do something that is aimed at all individuals equally	All bills **shall** be paid in cash.
Making a prophecy	When you are older, you **shall** marry a rich woman.
To issue a formal instruction	You **shall** all meet in the town square at 6 am.

Notes

CAN (CANNOT OR CAN'T)

This modal is mostly used to talk about present ability; use the modal 'could' when referring to a past ability – one that is no longer possessed (I **could** run a mile in 5 minutes when I was 19).

There are two forms for the negative version: **can't**, which is usually used in speech to indicate regret at not being able to do something (I'm sorry I **can't** come with you) and **cannot**, which is used to place an emphasis on the unwillingness (I **cannot** stand that man) or inability (I **cannot** make it start whatever I do) to do something.

When used in questions **Can I…** is not considered as polite as asking May I…? ('May I have your name please' is better than 'Can I have your name please?'). For example, 'May I have your name please', would be used by someone like a receptionist or maitre d'; whereas, '**Can** I have your name please', would be used by someone in authority like a policeman. Generally, you would use **can** when asking for some physical action, involving movement, is to be performed (Don't use '~~May you open the door please?~~', use '**Can** you open the door please?' instead).

Use for	Sample sentences
Ask about ability	**Can** you speak English?
Ask about possibility	**Can** you pass me the salt please?
Asking permission (formal)	**Can** I go to the bathroom?
Giving Permission	Yes, you **can** go to the bathroom.
Express confidence	You **can** do it.
Indicate prohibitions	You **can't** go in there, the floor is wet.
General possibility	I think scientists **can** find a cure for cancer.
Provide choices	You **can** go with me or stay at home.
Discuss opportunities	With those grades you **can** study for your Master's degree.
Future probability	There **can** be peace in the Middle East.
Detect with senses (hear, smell, touch, taste and see)	**Can** you hear that noise? *or* I **can** see the sea *or* I **can** smell dead fish.
Anger (negative form)	You **cannot** be serious.

OUGHT TO (OUGHT NOT)

This modal is mostly used to give suggestions for future actions. There are various negative forms of this modal: **Ought not** is regarded as the standard or correct version;. **Oughtn't**, usually in the spoken form, is found in some parts of the United States; **Hadn't ought** is a common spoken form in some northern areas of the USA and **Didn't ought** and **Shouldn't ought** are sometimes used in the spoken form. In writing, unless it is fictional writing using colloquial English dialogue, **Oughtn't** or **Ought not** (emphatic version) should be used.

Only the positive form of this modal is followed by the infinitive version of the main verb - the negative versions are followed by a simple verb.

Use for	Sample sentences
To express an ideal behaviour	People of all races **ought to** be treated equally.
To express a moral obligation	You **ought to** set a good example to your children.
To say why	It **ought to** be good as it cost a lot.
To express approval	He **ought to** be rewarded for helping her like that.
To express duty	Every citizen **ought to** help.
To express indignation about a lack of morals	He **ought to** be ashamed of himself cheating like that.
To express a just punishment	He **ought to** be put in prison for what he did.
To express probability	They **ought to** be here soon.
To express the sensible thing to do	You **ought to** be home before dark.
To show an occurrence if certain conditions are met	It **ought to** be a nice day today if it doesn't rain.
To suggest a good idea	You really **ought not to** be doing that.
To suggest a natural consequence	It **ought to** have rained last night according to the weather forecast.
To suggest appropriate action	You **ought to** take your wife out to dinner on your anniversary.
To suggest the best course of action	You really **ought to** give up smoking.

SHOULD (SHOULDN'T)

This modal is mainly used to express duty, necessity or obligation. It is commonly regarded as the past version of the modal 'shall'. It is commonly used in the subjunctive (I **shouldn't** touch that wire if I were you, you might get a shock!).

Use for	Sample sentences
To express duty	You **should** put your family before everyone else.
To express necessity - in the form of personal advice	You **should** register if you want to attend.
To express a moral obligation	You **should** do it for the good of the team.
Describe an ideal behaviour	You **shouldn't** tell lies.
Official orders expressed as suggestions	Passengers **should** proceed to gate 3 concourse 1.
To solicit (ask for) or give advise	**Should** I wear the black dress or the blue one? (Solicit) You **shouldn't** wear either. (Give)
To express past regret	I **should** have studied harder when I was at school.
To reply to an enquiry about how a person feels (in the form of a question)	Question: Are you ok? Answer: Why **shouldn't** I be OK?

Notes

WOULD (WOULDN'T)

This modal is mainly used to express wishes or requests. It is regarded as the past version of the modal 'will'. It is often used in the subjunctive (I wouldn't do that if I were you!). It is analogous to the modal 'should'.

Use for	Sample sentences
After 'wish', to show regret or irritation over someone's refusal or actions	I wish you **would** come with me, it's going to be a great show *or* I wish you **wouldn't** do that, it's annoying me.
Future in the past	At University I **would** study every night.
In indirect (or reported) speech	He told me that he **would** speak to you later.
Indicate distance from present circumstances	I **would** be in London by now if I didn't have to wait for you.
Indicate imagined situations	If I were rich I **would** buy a yacht.
Indicate unreal situations	What **would** have happened if I hadn't come?
Polite offers	**Would** you like a lift to the station?
Polite requests (a 'softer' form of will)	**Would** you mind holding this for me please?
Talking about past habits	When I was living in England I **would** buy a newspaper every morning.
To express a wish (it is used instead of say "I wish…")	**Would** that he had told us before we started out. (Formal or idiomatic)
To express an intention or inclination	I **would** want to have my own key if I lived here (intention) *or* I **would** prefer it wasn't so loud (inclination).
To express concession	It **would** appear that he is correct.
To express repeated actions in the past	I **would** get up at 5 am every morning to go for a run.
To express the future in positive and negative past tense sentences	I said I **would** go tomorrow *or* She said she **wouldn't** do it, but did it anyway.
To soften a statement	That **would** be intolerable.

MAY (MAY NOT)

This modal is often used to indicate that there is an even chance (50%) of an action either taking place or not taking place, therefore **may** and **may not** essentially have the same meaning. Use the positive 'may' in optimistic sentences and use the negative 'may not' in pessimistic sentences. It is considered to be very polite when used in a question as it implies that the listener has the choice of agreeing or disagreeing and the speaker would not be offended with whatever the listener decides.

Use for	Sample sentences
Ask for something politely	**May** I see your invitation?
Polite greeting to clients or visitors	How **may** I help you?
To seek permission	**May** I leave the room please?
To indicate permission	Yes, you **may** take the car today.
To indicate pessimism	I **may not** pass my exams.
To indicate (~50%) possibility	It **may** rain this afternoon.
To express irrelevance in spite of certain or likely truth	I **may not** be clever but at least I can swim.
Talking about the past with uncertainty	I **may** have been mistaken. (Past perfect)
Talking about the present with uncertainty	I **may** be wrong of course. (Present simple with be)
Talking about the future with uncertainty	Liverpool **may** win the cup. (Future simple with be)
Talking about things that can happen in certain situations	If Manchester United loses we **may** still win the championship.
To indicate purpose	He gave his life so others **may** live.
To give good reason for a reaction (idiomatic)	You **may** well ask *or* You **may** as well know that…
To indicate someone do something, because there is no reason to do anything else	If the band has finished playing then I **may** as well go home.
To express a wish or prayer.	**May** you live long and prosper.
To express good wishes, for example at a wedding (idiomatic)	**May** all your troubles be little ones (meaning the only problems you have in your marriage will come from having children).

MIGHT (MIGHT NOT)

This modal is often used to indicate that there is only a slight possibility (around 30%) of something happening. It is often regarded as the past version of the modal **may** and is used in a similar way in framing questions and indicating possibility, particularly in UK English.

Use for	Sample sentences
Expressing something that is unlikely in response to an unlikely possible outcome	You **might** win an Oscar and pigs **might** fly.
In formal questions (usually followed by a reason for the request).	**Might** I be excused from the lecture today? I have to visit my sick mother.
Indicating a possible event	I heard this **might** well be their last concert.
Making a polite request (primarily in UK English)	**Might** I ask who is calling please?
Making a polite suggestion (UK English)	If you don't like it here, you **might** be better off moving.
Past purpose	I asked for your names so I **might** check your details.
Saying that something was possible, but did not actually happen	It was really frightening. We **might** have been killed.
Stating a past possibility, especially one that is very unlikely to have happened	I **might** have been a rock star if I hadn't become a teacher.
Telling someone they have not done something they should have done	You **might** have told me it was raining out here.
To express advisability	You **might** want to thank him for helping us with this.
Indicate what the speaker believes is a good reason for a reaction	The bad weather **might** be being caused by global warming.
To indicate that another action would have been better	This is so boring, I **might** as well have stayed at home
To understate certainty (particularly in ironic statements)	I **might** be wrong but I think she is annoyed with you.
To express exasperation at finding out who did something - usually bad	I **might** have known you were behind it.

Verb Types

COULD (COULDN'T)

This modal is often used to give a phrase a doubtful or subjunctive meaning. It is also used as the past version of can. When forming questions, the speaker is fairly doubtful they will get an affirmative answer (in other words they doubt the person being asked will say 'yes'). It is also used to give reasons for not doing something, together with the conjunction 'but' (I **could** have gone out <u>but</u> it was raining).

Note that the negative 'couldn't' is commonly used in speech. The full version, 'could not' is used, both in speech and text, to emphasize that the reason the action hadn't been done was because it was impossible to do.

Use for	Sample sentences
An unlikely possibility	A meteorite **could** hit you tomorrow.
Ask a question expecting a negative answer	**Could** I borrow some money?
Making an unreasonable request (Ironic in UK English)	**Could** I borrow your life savings as I have a great stock market tip.
Emphasizing feelings	I'm so happy I **could** sing.
Expressing a less favourable action (possibly with reason why)	I **could** go to the dance with him, but only if no-one else asks me.
Expressing regret at choosing a particular course of action	I **could** have married a rich man instead I married a failure.
Expressing wistful regret	I **could** have been a star.
Give reason for not doing something (with **have** *and* **but**)	I **could have** watched the program **but** I was at a party.
Indicate anger at someone's action (**could** is emphasised)	How **could** you be so stupid?
Less certain of abilities	I'm not sure I **could** write a book.
Giving an alternative suggestion	You **could** always go to the doctor.
Making polite requests	**Could** you tell me the time please?
Past capabilities (past version of **can**)	She **could** run a mile in 4 minutes at one time but not now.
Possible action in response to a previous action	If you had saved enough money you **could** afford to go on holiday.
Reluctant possibility	I **could** go I suppose.
Talk about exceptional ability	She **could** read by the age of three.

TENSE, ASPECT AND MOOD

Before moving on to how tenses are created let us take have a look at what constitutes a tense. According to grammarians, a verb structure is made up of "tense (location in time), aspect (fabric of time – a single block of time, continuous flow of time, or repetitive occurrence), and mood or modality (degree of necessity, obligation, probability, ability)."[1] In other words, a verb structure says whether the **timing** is important (tense) **when**, how long it took and how often it happens (aspect) and the **possibility** of it happening (modality).

In order to study how this works let's look at a sample sentence:

I may attend on Saturday.

The ***verb structure*** tells us:

Tense: the structure indicates a simple future event and in this case the **timing** is important.

Aspect: the use of simple future means **when** it will happen needs to be specified, which is the reason for the prepositional phrase 'on Saturday'.

Modality: the modal verb 'may' indicates that there is a notional 50% **possibility** of it happening.

In general we don't consider them separately; instead, we simply refer to them collectively as the 'tense' of the verb.

Notes

---

[1] Bybee, Joan L., Revere Perkins, and William Pagliuca (1994) The Evolution of Grammar: Tense, Aspect, and Modality in the Languages of the World. University of Chicago Press

FUNCTIONS OF VERB TENSES

Verb tenses can be complex to understand and so they are presented in a number of different ways in this book in order to aid in your comprehension of them. The tables below show, in a simplified form, what the tenses are used for in terms of time or results.

The top row explains the motivation of the tense in simple terms.

Expressing Moment (Simple Tense)		
An action that takes place one or more times, may never happen or for describing sequential or repetitive actions or facts		
Simple past	**Simple present**	**Simple future**
He **worked** until 8 every night	He **works** until 8 every night	He **will work** until 8 every night

It is the simplest of the verb tenses as it refers (in the past and future versions) to single events that have happened (simple past) or are going to happen (simple future). The most common uses for the simple present are in talking about repetitive, but separate, actions or in stating facts.

Expressing Period (Continuous /Progressive Tense)		
An continuous action going on at that moment or multiple actions taking place at the same time		
Past continuous	**Present continuous**	**Future continuous**
He **was working** hard while she **was cooking**	He **is working** hard while she **is cooking**	He **will be working** and she **will be cooking**

This tense is mainly used to talk about something that happens over a period of time. When it is used to talk about simultaneous actions if the second person's action is not as important as the first person's, use the simple tense to describe the second action. **Examples:** Both actions equally important "I **am reading** while she **is writing**" and where the second action is not as important "I **was reading** while she **slept**". This tense is referred to as **continuous** in UK English and **progressive** in US English.

FUNCTIONS OF VERB TENSES

Functions continued...

Expressing Results (Perfect Tense)

An action taking place before or beyond a certain moment in time with an emphasis on the result

Past Perfect Simple	Present Perfect Simple	Future Perfect Simple
He **had worked** hard until he was ill	He **has** always **worked** hard up to now	He **will have worked** hard by the end of today

This tense is primarily used to express achievements, experiences and possession. It is the only tense that doesn't need any sort of time marker (for example it doesn't usually matter when you did or obtained something, what was important is that you did or have it).

Expressing Duration (Perfect Continuous Tense)

To express the length of time something has gone on or will be going on for

Past perfect continuous	Present perfect continuous	Future perfect continuous
He **had been working** here for ten years.	He **has been working** here for ten years.	He **will have been working** here for ten years.
Followed by the reason that he no longer works there or the time he left.	At this moment the condition is still true and has been for a while.	Followed by the marker date (by July next year) or event (by Christmas).

This is the least commonly used tense and is mainly used to say how long an action has been happening for. It is usually followed by the preposition since (indicating when the action started) or for (indicating how long the action has been going on for). All 3 tenses can refer to something that started in the past, the difference being whether the action has finished already (past perfect continuous), is still going on and there is no known limit to how long it will last (present perfect continuous) or that it is due to finish at, or will be counted up to, some specified point in the future.

INTRANSITIVE VERBS

Intransitive verbs do not need an object but can be followed by prepositional phrases, adverbs, adverb clauses, adjectives and adjective clauses. They should not be used in the passive voice, unless they are being used as part of a phrasal verb. In the table below, which contains some of the most commonly used intransitive verbs, the R denotes a regular verb and I denotes an irregular verb.

Verb		3rd Person	Past Simple	Present part.	Past Part.
agree	R	agrees	agreed	agreeing	agreed
appear	R	appears	appeared	appearing	appeared
arrive	R	arrives	arrived	arriving	arrived
become	I	becomes	became	become	become
belong	R	belongs	belonged	belonging	belonged
consist	R	consists	consisted	consisting	consisted
cough	R	coughs	coughed	coughing	coughed
cry	R	cries	cried	crying	cried
die	R	dies	died	dying	died
disappear	R	disappears	disappeared	disappearing	disappeared
emerge	R	emerges	emerged	emerging	emerged
endure	R	endures	endured	enduring	endured
exist	R	exists	existed	existing	existed
fall	I	falls	fell	falling	fallen
happen	R	happens	happened	happening	happened
inquire	R	inquires	inquired	inquiring	inquired
laugh	R	laughs	laughed	laughing	laughed
live	R	lives	lived	living	lived
look	R	looks	looked	looking	looked
respond	R	responds	responded	responding	responded
sit	I	sits	sat	sitting	sat
sleep	I	sleeps	slept	sleeping	slept
smile	R	smiles	smiled	smiling	smiled
sneeze	R	sneezes	sneezed	sneezing	sneezed
stand	I	stands	stood	standing	stood
stay	R	stays	stayed	staying	stayed
wait	R	waits	waited	waiting	waited

TRANSITIVE VERBS

Transitive verbs are verbs that always require an object in order to create a grammatically correct sentence. The object can be a noun, noun phrase, noun clause, pronoun, infinitive and, in some cases (e.g. abstract verbs), an adjective. The following table contains some of the most commonly used transitive verbs. Note, I stands for an Irregular verb and R stands for a Regular verb.

Verb		3rd Person	Past Simple	Present part.	Past Part.
answer	R	answers	answered	answering	answered
break	I	breaks	broke	breaking	broken
bring	I	brings	brought	bringing	brought
buy	I	buys	bought	buying	bought
catch	I	catches	caught	catching	caught
cost	I	costs	cost	costing	cost
drink	I	drinks	drank	drinking	drunk
get	I	gets	got	getting	got
give	I	gives	gave	giving	given
help	R	helps	helped	helping	helped
learn	R	learns	learned	learning	learned
leave	I	leaves	left	leave	left
lend	I	lends	lent	lending	lent
make	I	makes	made	making	made
offer	R	offers	offered	offering	offered
owe	R	owes	owed	owing	owed
pay	I	pays	paid	paying	paid
play	R	plays	played	playing	played
promise	R	promises	promised	promising	promised
read	I	reads	read	read	read
see	I	sees	saw	seeing	seen
send	I	sends	sent	sending	sent
show	I	shows	showed	showing	shown
take	I	takes	took	taking	taken
teach	I	teaches	taught	teaching	taught
tell	I	tells	told	telling	told
walk	R	walks	walked	walking	walked

Verb Tenses

IRREGULAR -V- REGULAR VERBS

Most verbs in English tend to have the past tense formed by having the suffix 'ed' (stay - stayed) or 'd' (love/loved if the verb ends in 'e') appended to them. These are referred to as regular verbs.

Other verbs do not follow this convention and are referred to as irregular verbs. These verbs were mainly derived from the Anglo-Saxon verbs that the early English people spoke. If you look at the list opposite, that shows all of the current irregular verbs, you will see that they represent the vocabulary that a mainly agrarian society would need. Anglo-Saxon has bequeathed a number of anomalies in English that have helped to make the language more complicated, such as the irregular nouns (where the plural form is not suffixed with 's': ox-oxen, fish-fish and sheep-sheep).

In dialectic speech some verbs have become irregular (or regular) or simply have a different irregular construct. These include:

Present Tense	UK English	Dialectical English
Dive	Dived	Dove
Drag	Dragged	Drug
Get	Got	Gotten
Hang	Hung	Hanged
Lie	Lay	Lain
Overload	Overloaded	Overladen
Show	Showed	Shown
Underlie	Underlain	Underlaid

It is worth noting that many of the irregular verbs have had their meaning changed by being appended with a prefix, such as:

Prefix	Meaning	Derived from
for(e)	Before	Preposition (Latin 'per')
inter	Between	Preposition (Latin)
mis	Wrong or badly	Adverb (Norse)
out	Beyond	Preposition (Old English)
over	Higher than	Preposition (Anglo Saxon 'uber')
re	Do again	Prefix (Latin)
under	Lower than	Preposition (Anglo Saxon)
with	Against	Preposition (Anglo Saxon - wiþ)

The following table contains all of the 260 current irregular verbs. Note, some of them are no longer commonly used.

Arise	Awake	Bear	Beat	Become	Befall	Beget
Begin	Behold	Bend	Beseech	Bestrew	Bestride	Bet
Bid	Bind	Bite	Bleed	Bless	Blow	Break
Breed	Bring	Broadcast	Build	Burn	Burst	Bust
Buy	Cast	Change	Choose	Cleave	Cling	Come
Cost	Creep	Cut	Deal	Do	Dig	Dive
Draw	Dream	Drink	Drive	Dwell	Eat	Fall
Feed	Feel	Fight	Find	Flee	Fling	Fly
Forbid	Forecast	Foresee	Forget	Forgive	Forego	Forgo
Forsake	Forswear	Freeze	Gainsay	Get	Gird	Give
Go	Grind	Hang	Have	Hear	Hew	Hide
Hit	Hold	Hurt	Input	Interbreed	Interweave	Keep
Kneel	Knit	Know	Lay	Lie (down)	Lead	Lean
Leap	Learn	Leave	Lend	Let	Light	Lose
Make	Mean	Meet	Mimic	Miscast	Mishear	Mislay
Mislead	Misspeak	Misspell	Misspend	Mistake	Misunderstand	Mow
Offset	Outbid	Outdo	Outfight	Outgrow	Outrun	Outsell
Outshine	Overbid	Overcome	Overdo	Overdraw	Overeat	Overhang
Overhear	Overlay	Overload	Overpay	Override	Overrun	Oversee
Overshoot	Oversleep	Overspend	Overtake	Overthrow	Overwrite	Partake
Pay	Plead	Preset	Prove	Put	Quit	Read
Rebuild	Recast	Refit	Remake	Rend	Repay	Rerun
Resit (UK)	Rethink	Rewrite	Rid (of)	Ride	Ring	Rise
Run	Saw	Say	See	Seek	Sell	Send
Set	Sew	Shake	Shear	Shed	Shine	Shoe
Shoot	Show	Shrink	Shut	Sing	Sink	Sit
Slay	Sleep	Slide	Sling	Slink	Slit	Smell
Smite	Sneak	Sow	Speak	Speed	Spell	Spend
Spill	Spin	Spit	Split	Spoil	Spotlight	Spread
Spring	Stand	Steal	Stick	Sting	Stink	Strew
Stride	Strike	String	Strive	Sublet	Swear	Sweep
Swell	Swim	Swing	Take	Teach	Tear	Tell
Think	Thrive	Throw	Thrust	Tread	Typecast	Unbend
Undercut	Undergo	Underlie	Underpay	Undersell	Understand	Undertake
Underwrite	Undo	Unwind	Uphold	Upset	Wake	Waylay
Wear	Weave	Wed	Weep	Wet	Win	Wind
Wind	Withdraw	Withhold	Withstand	Wreak	Wring	Write

Verb Tenses

CONDITIONALS

Conditional clauses: are sentences or phrases which impose a condition on the outcome. There are four types of conditional clause. The present conditional tense is used to describe a situation now that isn't true or isn't happening or couldn't possibly happen. This strange tense is only used in conditionals. The clause that contains it uses the modals **would, could, might,** or **should** and it may use the present conditional version of **be**, in that it takes the form **were**, irrespective of what pronoun or noun precedes it. For **Example: I wouldn't do that...** followed by the present conditional phrase ... **if I were you.**

Zero conditional

There are no conditions therefore what is said is a fact. It uses the present simple tense. The time is either always or now. It can be used to express:

Facts: If something is factual then there are no conditions.
Example: If you put your hand into boiling water you'll get scalded.

Negative facts: They can also be used to express negative facts.
Example: If you don't put fuel into an engine it will not run.

First conditional

First conditionals are used where it is both possible and also very likely that the condition will be fulfilled. They can be used to make statements or frame questions. The tense in the 'if' clause is the **simple present,** and the tense in the main clause is the **simple future.**

Using if: First conditionals can use the word **if** and the present simple tense

Example: If you come to my shop, I'll give you your money back.

Using will: you can also use the word **will** to create the clause to express certainty about something in the future.

Examples:
What will you do when you quit your job?
You will improve your English language skills by speaking to other people in English.

Second Conditional

Second conditionals are used where it is possible but also very unlikely that the condition will be fulfilled. The tense in the **'if'** clause is the **simple past**, and the tense in the main clause is the **present conditional. Using if and simple past:** the conditional clause uses **if** and the main clause uses **would** plus an infinitive - note that you would usually use the subjunctive verb **'were'** even if the pronoun is I, he, she or it

Example: If I **were** rich, I would move away from here.

Third Conditional

Third conditionals: are used where it is impossible that the condition will be fulfilled because it refers to the past. The tense in the **'if'** clause is the **past perfect**, and the tense in the main clause is the **perfect conditional:** Note that the facts are the *opposite* of what is expressed, and they refer to an unreal past condition and its probable past result.

Example: If you hadn't eaten that oyster you wouldn't have been sick

Another type of 'if' sentence also exists, where the tense in the 'if' clause is past perfect, and the tense in the main clause is present conditional:

Examples:

If you **had taken** the right turning we wouldn't be lost now.
If I **had been** more successful I'd be rich now.
If you **hadn't been** so angry you'd still have your job.

Using Past Perfect Passive

Past perfect passive can be used together with 'if' to show that if a condition had been met then the outcome would have been different:

Example: If I had been asked then I would have bought some food on my way home. (Passive voice).

The question form of past perfect passive can also be used to express outcomes that are no longer possible:

Examples:
Had I been asked I would have told you that it wouldn't work.
Had I known it would rain I wouldn't have come.

SUBJUNCTIVE MOOD

Before moving onto describing the subjunctive we need to answer the question 'what is the **mood?**'

Put simply, the **mood** is the form a verb takes to show whether it should be regarded as a fact, is in the form of a command, is being used to express uncertainty or possibility or to express a wish, suggestion or desire. These moods are expressed in the following ways:

The Indicative Mood. This mood is used to state facts or to ask questions. This form uses 'standard' verb tenses such as the continuous tense. For **Example:**

He is **singing** a song.   (Stating a fact)
Is he **singing** a song? (Asking a question)

The Imperative Mood. This mood is used to give a command, to make a request or to demand something. This mood commonly uses the second person (you), either in the singular or plural form, as the subject, which is often omitted when the order is given. Exclamation marks are often used to add stress. For **Example:**

Please **sing** a song (Request prefaced with the softening adverb 'please')
Sing a song! (Command, stressed with an exclamation mark).
You! Sing a song! (Demand, where **you** is being used an indicative - usually together with finger pointing - followed by the imperative).

The Indeterminate Mood. This mood, which is unique to CORE English, is used to express uncertainty or possibility. This is a very common mood and is expressed using a suitable modal verb. In fact the very word modal means "*of or denoting the mood [of the verb]*", showing that is one of the main reasons for using this type of verb. For example, study the following four examples which express increasing levels of doubt:

He **will** sing a song (>50% possibility)
He **may** sing a song (50% possibility)
He **might** sing a song (<50% possibility)
He **will not** sing a song (0% possibility)

SUBJUNCTIVE MOOD

The Subjunctive Mood: This mood is used when a condition is considered to be doubtful or not factual. It is commonly found in conditional clauses beginning with the word **if** and in clauses following a verb that expresses demands, judgements, opinions, proposals, suggestions, regrets, requests or wishes. It takes the form of 2nd person verb form for 3rd person singular (no 's' or 'es'), **'be'** instead of **'am, is** or **are'** for the present and **'were'** instead of **'was'** for the past.

In 'if' statements it is used for suggestions or impossible conditions

I wouldn't make her angry **if** I *were* you. (Suggestion)

If I *were* younger I'd run faster than you. (Impossible condition)

It would be mainly used with the following verbs:

Verb	Example sentence
ask	I **asked** if it *were* possible that he'd sing.
demand	I **demand** he *be* made to sing.
determine	We **determined** that they *be* held liable.
insist	I **insisted** she *be* home before dark.
move	The tribunal **moved** he *be* struck off.
order	The judge **ordered** he *be* remanded in custody.
pray	I **prayed** she *be* cured.
prefer	I **prefer** she *take* her business elsewhere.
recommend	I **recommended** she *see* a psychiatrist.
regret	She **regretted** she *were* not younger.
request	I **requested** that he *were* present at the meeting.
require	The court **requires** he *answer* the question.
suggest	I **suggest** you *be* careful with that knife.
wish	I **wish** I *were* taller.

It would also be used in clauses following adjectives of necessity	
crucial	It is **crucial** *that it **be** fixed on time.*
desirable	It is **desirable** *that you **be** properly dressed.*
essential	It is **essential** *that you **be** in the match on Saturday.*
imperative	It is **imperative** *that the contract **be** signed today.*
important	It is **important** *that I **be** given the facts.*
vital	It is **vital** *it **be** kept secret until the launch.*

QUESTION FORMATION

The structure of most questions in English, aside from questions posed using a rising tone at the end of the phrase, follow the same simple format. This is represented by the diagram on the right and consists of swapping the positions of the verb and the subject. This process is called 'inversion'.

Only certain verbs can be inverted: **be, have** and **modal verbs.** With other other verbs the inversion would be replaced with **do.** Note, the 'not' in negative verb forms does not move. For **Example:**

Verb	Statement	Inversion	Question
Be	*She* is hot		**Is** *she* hot?
Have	*He* **has** eaten		**Has** *he* eaten?
Modal	*It* **will** bite		**Will** *it* bite?
Other	*You* **like** skiing		**Do** *you* **like** skiing?
Not	*He* **is not** hot		**Is** *he* **not** hot?

Simple inversion questions are mostly used to find the state of someone/something. Other types of questions can be used to find other types of words, but they still use the same inversion form. For **Example:**

Who **is** <u>that girl</u>? (*Pronoun* question word to get a noun answer - note the subject is '<u>that girl</u>' so the statement would be '<u>That girl</u> **is**...').

What colour **do** you **like**? (*Adjective/determiner* question word to get a specifying adjective or noun phrase answer from a group).

When **are** you **leaving**? (*Adverb* question word to find when, where, how, how much or how often).

To whom **should I send** it? (Prepositional phrase question form to get a noun - it can be regarded as a very specific pronoun question).

Even tag questions follow the same inversion, but instead of being prefaced with the inverted format the inversion is placed at the end, after a comma, usually with the verb in the negative format.

You will be going with us, **<u>won't</u>** <u>*you*</u>? (<u>Inverted form</u> at the end).

If the initial phrase is negative the inverted verb will be positive.

He isn't coming with us, <u>**is** *he*</u> ?

SUBJECT/VERB AGREEMENT

One of the most common mistakes that English language learners make is in not making the verb agree with the subject.

The general rule, for singular subjects, is that a 3rd person singular subject (such as **he, she, it** or a noun) would have an 's' suffixed to the verb (He go**es** to school every day). Note that this may take the form of '**es**' with verbs ending in '**ch**', '**s**', '**sh**', '**x**', or '**z**' , for example, hatch**es**, hiss**es**, mash**es**, mix**es** or buzz**es**. In addition, verbs ending with a '**y**' (such as **fly**) form the third-person singular by changing the **y** to **ies** (**flies**).

The 3rd person plural (**they** and plural nouns), on the other hand, generally take the same form as the 1st person plural (**we**), for **Example:** we **are** here *and* they **are** there.

The most common verb uses are outlined below.

With a combined pronoun and noun subject: if the subject is comprised of a *pronoun* and a <u>noun</u> joined by the conjunction 'and' (meaning both) then use the plural verb.

Example: <u>Jiraporn</u> and *I* **are** both here.

With a combined subject comprised of two nouns: if the sentence is composed of two or more nouns using the conjunction 'and', then use a plural verb.

Example: <u>Fred</u> and <u>Alice</u> **are** here

With a combined subject comprised of two singular pronouns: if the sentence is composed of two or more pronouns using the conjunction 'and', then use a plural verb. Note that the first person singular pronoun comes last.

Example: Both *her* and *I* **were** there.

With an alternative subject comprised of two nouns: if the sentence is composed of two or more nouns using the conjunction 'or', offering a choice, then use a singular verb.

Example: Either <u>Jiraporn</u> or <u>Fred</u> need**s** to be here to open up.

SUBJECT/VERB AGREEMENT

With a negative sentence comprised of two nouns: if the sentence is negative and composed of two or more nouns using the conjunction 'nor' then use a plural verb.

Example: Neither <u>Jiraporn</u> nor <u>Fred</u> **were** there.

With an alternative subject comprised of two pronouns: if the sentence is composed of two or more nouns using the conjunction 'or', offering a choice, then use a singular verb.

Example: *He* or *she* **is** here - *You* or *I* **are** going.

With a combined compound subject containing both a singular and a plural noun: if the nouns that form the subject are joined by 'and', the verb will always be plural. This rule also applies to a mixture of singular and plural pronouns.

Examples:
Both the <u>students</u> and the <u>teacher</u> **are** here.
(Singular noun closest to the verb).
Both the <u>teacher</u> and the <u>students</u> **are** here.
(Plural noun closest to the verb).

With an alternate compound subject containing both a singular and a plural noun: if the nouns that form the subject are joined by 'or', the verb should agree with the part of the subject that is nearer the verb. This rule also applies to a mixture of singular and plural pronouns.

Examples:
Either the <u>students</u> or the <u>teacher</u> **is** here.
(Singular noun closest to the verb).
Either the <u>teacher</u> or the <u>students</u> **are** here.
(Plural noun closest to the verb).

With 'wh' question words: when using question words choose the verb depending on the expected answer. So if the answer is likely to be singular then use a singular verb.

Examples:
What **is** her name?   Singular expected answer
What **are** their names?   Plural expected answer

SUBJECT/VERB AGREEMENT

With an alternate compound subject containing both a singular and a plural noun: if the nouns that form the subject are joined by 'nor', the verb will be plural even if the singular noun is closer to the verb. This rule also applies to a mixture of singular and plural pronouns.

Examples:
Neither the <u>students</u> nor the <u>teacher</u> **are** here: the singular is closest
Neither the <u>teacher</u> nor the <u>students</u> **are** here: the plural is closest

Where a phrase comes between the subject and the verb: if a phrase comes between the subject and a verb, the verb must match the original subject.

Examples:
The *teacher*, plus all of his students, **is** going to the museum.
The *students*, together with the teacher, **are** going to the museum.

With pronouns, or determiners, referring to a singular object, or a person, within a group: When using pronouns such as **each, either, neither, everyone, everybody, anybody, anyone, nobody, somebody, someone,** and **no one** use a singular verb.

Examples:

Each person **needs** to bring a packed lunch.	**Determiner**
Each **is** responsible for his own equipment.	**Pronoun**
Either person **is** suitable.	**Determiner**
Either **is** fine with me.	**Pronoun**
Neither one **suits** me.	**Determiner**
Neither **is** suitable.	**Pronoun**
Everyone **is** invited.	**Pronoun**
Everybody **has** signed the form.	**Pronoun**
Does *anybody* here speak English?	**Pronoun**
Is *anyone* suspected of the crime?	**Pronoun**
Nobody **likes** cleaning.	**Pronoun**
Somebody **knows** about this.	**Pronoun**
Someone **is** making a lot of money.	**Pronoun**
No one **is** coming to help us.	**Pronoun**

SUBJECT/VERB AGREEMENT

With plural nouns that refer to singular objects: some objects, although singular, are represented by plural nouns (they would usually be prefaced with **a pair of…**). In these cases use a plural verb.

Examples:

Those *scissors* **are** really sharp.
The new *tweezers* **are** very precise.
These *pliers* **are** used for fine work.
Trousers, not *shorts*, **are** needed for work.
Knickers **are** called *panties* in the USA.
These *underpants* **are** too tight.
The *shears* **are** used for pruning branches.
My wire *cutters* **are** getting blunt.

When using the negative of do: **don't** is the contraction of the singular 1st and 2nd person or plural negative **'do not'** and **doesn't** is the contraction of the third person negative **'does not'**. Use don't with a singular object and doesn't with a plural object.

Examples:

I **don't** like her.	1st person singular
You **don't** like her, do you?	2nd person singular
We **don't** like her.	1st person plural
They **don't** like her either.	3rd person plural
She **doesn't** like any of us.	3rd person singular

With certain specialist nouns: specialist nouns representing seemingly plural currencies, subjects and diseases, use singular verbs even though they are expressed in the form of plural nouns.

Examples:

One hundred *pounds* **is** all you need to buy a ticket.[1]
Mathematics **is** hard for many people.
Measles **is** on the increase as parents reject the MMR vaccination.

---

[1] Many Asian currencies are not followed by a plural 's' (Yuan, Yen and Baht), while most western currencies are (Dollars, Pounds and Euros)

SUBJECT/VERB AGREEMENT

With uncountable nouns: use a singular verb with uncountable nouns.

Examples:

The *news* **is** on the TV at 6 p.m.
The *furniture* **is** being delivered today.
This *rice* **is** stone cold.
That *water* **looks** polluted.
Some *money* **is** better than no money.
Is there any *milk* left in the fridge?

With collective nouns representing more than one person: nouns that represent groups are usually regarded as being singular and need a singular noun:

Examples:

The group of *girls* **is** visiting today.
The football *team* **is** playing away.
The *committee* **has** decided to recommend some changes.
The *class* **has** decided to buy their teacher a gift.
My *family* **is** getting together at Christmas.

With an individual from within a group: When talking about a singular entity from within a group use a singular verb. The group can be referred to using a prepositional phrase (see the first example) or using a possessive noun (second example).

Examples:

The *CEO* of the company **is** here. (Simple verb)
The team's *quarterback* **set up** the win. (Phrasal verb)

With multiple entities from within a group: The convention when talking about multiple entities in a group is if they differ in some way from the others in a group use a plural verb - if they are the same, particularly if their unanimity is being stressed, use a singular verb.

Examples:

The club *committee* **are** not in agreement. (Differing views)
The club *committee* **is** in agreement (Their views are the same)

TENSE MEANINGS AND USES

On the following pages you will see the construction methodology of the various tenses and what they are used for.

The tenses each have their own page (12 active voice tenses and 12 passive voice tenses), as do 'be' and the modals. You can either write your own sentences or you can search using the special search tool on the website, using the structure and the verb of your choice, to find a suitable sentence. It is recommended that you also write down what function the tense is playing in the sentence (for example, with present simple active it may be describing repeated actions or stating facts).

The page structure for each tense is all follows:

TENSE BEING DISCUSSED

Creation: This describes how the tense is formed. It lists both the mandatory parts (like the main/descriptive verb) and the optional parts (like the negative version). This will be followed by both negative and positive examples.

Structural Usage: This would be followed by usage notes on the tense, for example how it is structured for special purposes, negative sentences and abbreviations. **Examples** of the relevant points will then follow.

Uses: The uses of the tense will then be given a separate line, together with at least one sample sentence. The use is in bold and the description and sample sentences are in normal text. Note the tense is highlighted in bold.

Comparisons: In some instances, or where confusion has been known to have arisen, then a section will appear at the foot of the page showing how the tense differs from another, similar, tense. Sample sentences, together with descriptions, are given for each.

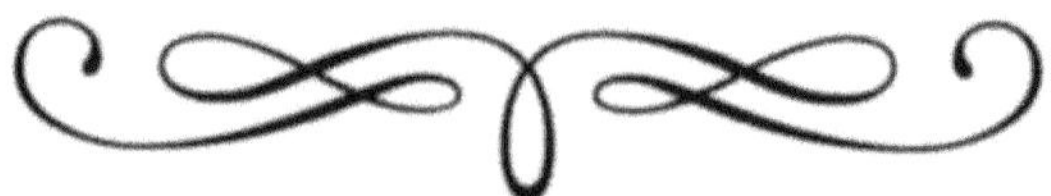

FORMING ACTIVE VERB TENSES

In this section you will see how each verb tense is created. Wherever possible the same main verbs and objects and/or prepositional phrases are used so you can focus on how the verb structure changes between the different types of tenses. The sample sentences always follow the same pattern:

1st singular	Refers to **the person who is speaking**
2nd singular	Refers to **the person being spoken to**
3rd (m) singular	Refers to a **known** male that is being spoken about
3rd (f) singular	Refers to a **known** female that is being spoken about
3rd (n) singular	Refers to a **known** thing that is being spoken about
3rd (noun) singular	Refers to a **named** person or thing
1st plural	Refers to a group **including the person speaking**
3rd plural	Refers to a **known** group being spoken about
3rd (nouns) plural	Refers to a group of **named** persons or things

Note: (m) = male, (f) = female, (n) = neutral or unknown

There are two forms of verb formation for each tense. The first form uses intransitive verbs, which do not need an object, so they are generally followed by prepositional phrases. The second form uses transitive verbs, which do require an object, so they are generally followed by nouns, noun phrases or pronouns.

Each tense formation occupies a single page after which there is an exercise page where you can create your own sentences and, if it forms part of teacher lead directed study, have them assessed, corrected and graded or, for self-study purposes, you can check the sentences you create via the free grammar checker on the website.

When forming your own sentences you can use suitable intransitive or transitive verbs from the tables on the facing pages. Alternatively you can use verbs from the other verb books in this series or from dictionaries. Dictionaries will usually follow the verb with a [T] meaning it is a transitive verb or an [I] meaning it is intransitive.

Note that some verbs can be both transitive and intransitive and the final verb forms of this section (future perfect continuous) use these types of verbs.

TENSE WORKSHEETS

The tense formation worksheets on the following pages have been designed to show the simplicity of the verb structures and how they can be changed from one tense to another.

To aid understanding they are presented in tables with examples of every person in positive, negative and question forms. Both intransitive and transitive verbs are included to show how they can be used with either prepositional phrases to add more information (intransitive) or with noun phrases to add an object (transitive).

The same verbs, or adjectives formed from the verbs, are used throughout to aid consistency and to show the changes required to transition from one tense to another. The philosophy of this is to give the student confidence is making the transitions by demonstrating how easy it is.

CORE methodology differs from 'traditional' English verb tense instruction in that it uses a verb | adjective construction instead of the more traditional auxiliary verb | main verb construct in order to both simplify matters and because it can be better explained as to why tenses are constructed the way they are.

Finally, the worksheets have been designed to allow the learner to construct their own sentences based on their contexts rather than ones chosen for them. These can be created by the teacher, when used in a classroom setting, to provide a reference or by the individual learner using the specialised search tool on the tools page of the website. An example of the formulation would, based on wanting to find a sentence containing the subject noun 'beach' with the passive voice present perfect tense construct (note, the descriptive/main verb is not included) as:

"beach" + "has been"

Which produced the result: "A crocodile **has been spotted** on a well known tourist **beach**".

For classroom work a very low cost workbook is available that include extended versions of the tense worksheets together with support information for stand alone or supervised work.

PRESENT SIMPLE USING BE

Creation: This is the simplest of tenses and is mainly used to describe the state the subject is in by using an adjective or provides a link between the subject and the object (usually a noun). It takes the form:

be   **not** (if negative)

Examples:

I **am** hot (state verb with adjective).

She **is not** hot (negative state verb with adjective).

I **am** the teacher (verb showing the link between the subject and object - in this case they are the same thing).

She **is not** the teacher (negative verb proving that there is NO link between the subject and the object).

Use this tense to describe the following:

To describe a mental, emotional or physical state. Note, this describes the state of the subject using an adjective.

Examples:

She **is** undecided.   (Mental state)
He **is** sad.   (Emotional state)
They **are** exhausted. (Physical state)

To categorically state facts: To confirm that something is definitely true or is provably untrue.

Examples:

The sun **is** 96,000,000 miles away.
Cambridge **is not** bigger than London.

To confirm that was was just stated or questioned is true: To confirm that what the previous speaker said is correct.

Example:

Do you have problems with this software crashing?
Yes, it **is** very unstable.

State the position of something in time or space. This construct uses 'be' as an intransitive verb together with a <u>prepositional phrase</u> to determine the position.

Examples:

The car **is** <u>in the garage</u>. (Position in place).
He **is not** <u>on time</u>. (Position in time).

SIMPLE PRESENT USING BE

This tense uses the simple verb 'be' as used with the various persons. In order to form meaningful sentences adjectives can be added, as shown below. Note that (noun) means a singular subject noun; whereas, (nouns) means it is a plural noun. Abbreviations are in parentheses ().

Person	Positive Form		Adjective
	Subject	Verb	
First singular	I	am ('m)	happy.
Second singular	You	are ('re)	sad.
Third male singular	He	is ('s)	clever.
Third female singular	She	is ('s)	beautiful.
Third neutral singular	It	is ('s)	smelly.
Third (noun) singular	(Noun)	is ('s)	intelligent.
First plural	We	are ('re)	angry.
Third plural	They	are ('re)	cold.
Third (nouns) plural	(Nouns)	are ('re)	late.
Person	Negative Form		Adjective
First singular	I	am not ('m not)	listening.
Second singular	You	are not (aren't)	tall.
Third male singular	He	is not (isn't)	stupid.
Third female singular	She	is not (isn't)	fat.
Third neutral singular	It	is not (isn't)	barking.
Third (noun) singular	(noun)	is not (isn't)	unhappy.
First plural	We	are not (aren't)	truthful.
Third plural	They	are not (aren't)	lying.
Third (nouns) plural	(nouns)	are not (aren't)	coming.
Person	Question Form		Adjective
First singular	Am I		driving?
Second singular	Are you		walking?
Third male singular	Is he		strong?
Third female singular	Is she		going?
Third neutral singular	Is it		digging?
Third (noun) singular	Is (noun)		sleeping?
First plural	Are we		funny?
Third plural	Are they		running?
Third (nouns) plural	Are (nouns)		sleepy?

USING BE WORKSHEET

Positive Form

I am

You are

He is

She is

It is

(Noun) is

We are

They are

(Nouns) are

Negative Form

I am not

You are not

He is not

She is not

It is not

(noun) is not

We are not

They are not

(Nouns) are not

Question Form

Am I

Are you

Is he

Is she

Is it

Is (noun)

Are we

Are they

Are (nouns)

Verb Tenses

PRESENT SIMPLE ACTIVE

Creation: In most cases this tense is used to describe current or repeated actions. It takes the form:

do (optional)	**not** (if negative)	**base form of verb**

Examples: I do work at home *or* **I do not like** spicy food.

Note that the **do** is normally used to add emphasis in positive statements and may be omitted, but it is always used in negative sentences. So the sentence above could read: **I work** at home.

For 3rd person singular subjects (He, She, It, Noun) then the auxiliary would take the form '*does*' or the main verb would have *s* added (unless it is an irregular verb) if *do* is not used.

Examples: Kelly **does not like** swimming *or* Tony **likes** golf.

Use this tense to describe the following:

Repeated Actions: Use the Simple Present to express the idea that an action is repeated or mundane. The action can be anything such as a habit, daily event or a scheduled event. It can also be something that someone often forgets to do.

Examples: I start at 9 a.m. every day *or* I always **forget** my wife's birthday.

Facts: It can be used to indicate that speaker believes what they are saying is true, whether it is or not.

Examples: Global warming **is** a myth *or* Scientists **are** always right.

Imminent scheduled events: Can be used to announce the imminent arrival, departure or occurrence of something. Note the contraction of does not into doesn't.

Examples: The concert **is** at 8 p.m. this evening *or* The exam **doesn't start** until this afternoon.

Something happening now: Can be used to announce an immediate event.

Examples: Now he **tells** me *or* **Do** you **have** the tickets with you?

Something that is not only happening now: Unlike repeated or habitual actions it will refer to events that could happen both now and in the future.

Example: We sometimes **meet** on Thursdays as well.

WITH INTRANSITIVE VERBS

This tense uses the simple verb form as used with the various persons. Intransitive verbs do not need an object to form sentences; however, prepositional phrases plus either adverbs or 2nd prepositional phrases, can be added, as shown below. Note that (noun) means a singular **noun** – like a **name** – whereas (nouns) means it is a plural noun - like **the students**.

Positive Form	Verb	Prepositional Phrases	
I	work	in a university	at the moment.
You	go	to the library	in the morning.
He	studies	in the study room	in the afternoons.
She	cries	in her room	at night.
It	sleeps	in its kennel	with the other dog.
(Noun)	runs	in the park	near the river.
We	ski	in the snow	at the ski resort.
They	walk	on the path	next to the road.
(Nouns)	learn	about their subject	from their books.
Negative Form	Verb	Prepositional Phrases	
I do not	drive	across town	in the morning.
You do not	cycle	across the campus	on your bicycle.
He does not	doze	in a chair	near the heater.
She does not	eat	at the cafeteria	in her school.
It does not	bark	at strangers	near his home.
(noun) does not	reach	across the table	for the salt.
We do not	climb	up the hills	in the national park.
They do not	look	at their books	in the morning.
(nouns) do not	serve	in the shop	after school.
Question Form	Verb	Prepositional Phrases	
Do I	eat	at your house	in the evening?
Do you	come	past my house	in the morning?
Does he	walk	up the stairs	after his class?
Does she	play	on her computer	at night?
Does it	chew	on a bone	in its kennel?
Does (noun)	walk	under a bridge	on his way home?
Do we	go	to the party	in the evening?
Do they	fly	on their holiday	on the 17th?
Do (nouns)	look	at their iPads	under their desks?

WITH TRANSITIVE VERBS

This tense uses the simple verb form as used with the various persons. Intransitive verbs do not need an object to form sentences; however, prepositional phrases plus either adverbs or 2nd prepositional phrases, can be added, as shown below. Note that (noun) means a singular **noun** – like a **name** – whereas (nouns) means it is a plural noun - like **the students**.

Subject	Verb	Noun Phrase	Preposition
I	buy	the newspaper	at the local shop.
You	see	the reports	from your boss.
He	eats	some noodles	at lunchtime.
She	sells	life insurance	from her office.
It	notices	the people	in the park.
(Noun)	rides	the bus	to the office.
We	take	the same route	in the morning.
They	spend	their evenings	in the coffee shop.
(Nouns)	study	the subject	in their books.
Subject	Verb	Noun Phrase	Preposition
I do not	do	the crossword	in the morning.
You do not	know	the answer	to my question.
He does not	bring	people	to the meeting.
She does not	love	her own body	at the moment.
It does not	like	the food	in its bowl.
(noun) does not	teach	the students	on Friday.
We do not	buy	French fries	at any time.
They do not	catch	the bus	in the morning.
(nouns) do not	attend	the meetings	in the office.
Subject	Verb	Noun Phrase	Preposition
Do I	have	the attention	of my class?
Do you	take	a shower	in the mornings?
Does he	write	his notes	during his class?
Does she	play	the cello	in the orchestra?
Does it	dig	holes	in the garden?
Does (noun)	watch	movies	after work?
Do we	attend	the party	at the club?
Do they	drive	their car	on the footpath?
Do (nouns)	find	the hidden posts	on the website?

PRESENT SIMPLE

Positive Form

I

You

He

She

It

We

They

Negative Form

I do not

You do not

He does not

She does not

It does not

does not

We do not

They do not

do not

Question Form

Do I

Do you

Does he

Does she

Does it

Does

Do we

Do they

Do

Verb Tenses

PAST SIMPLE USING BE

Creation: This is the simplest of tenses and is mainly used to describe the state the subject was in by using an adjective or provides a previous link between the subject and the object (usually a noun).

be	not (if negative)

Examples:

I **was** hot (state verb with adjective)

She **was not** hot (negative state verb with adjective)

I **was** the teacher (verb showing the link between the subject and object - in this case they are the same thing)

She **was not** the teacher (negative verb proving that there was **NO** link between the subject and the object).

We **were** happy (positive verb showing the link to our emotional state).

They **were not** happy (negative verb showing that was no link to the their desired emotional state).

Use this tense to describe the following:

To describe a mental, emotional or physical state that is no longer true. Note, this describes the state of the subject using an adjective.

Examples:

She **was** undecided.   (Mental state)
He **was** sad.   (Emotional state)
They **were** exhausted. (Physical state)

To categorically state facts that used to be true: To confirm that something was once true or has been proven to be untrue.

Examples:

Rangoon **was** the capital of Burma.
Cambridge **was not** the first university in the UK.

State the past position of something in time or space. This construct uses '**be**' as an intransitive verb together with a <u>prepositional phrase</u> to determine a previous position.

Examples:

The car **was** <u>in the garage</u>. (Position in place)
He **was not** <u>on time</u>. (Position in time).

PAST SIMPLE USING BE

This tense uses the simple verb 'be' as used with the various persons. In order to form meaningful sentences adjectives are usually added, as shown below. Note that (noun) means a singular subject noun; whereas, (nouns) means it is a plural noun. Abbreviations are in brackets [ ].

Person	Positive Form		Adjective
	Subject	Verb	
First singular	I	was	happy.
Second singular	You	were	sad.
Third male singular	He	was	clever.
Third female singular	She	was	beautiful.
Third neutral singular	It	was	smelly.
Third (noun) singular	(Noun)	was	intelligent.
First plural	We	were	angry.
Third plural	They	were	cold.
Third (nouns) plural	(Nouns)	were	Late.

Person	Negative Form		Adjective
First singular	I	was not [wasn't]	listening.
Second singular	You	were not [weren't]	tall.
Third male singular	He	was not [wasn't]	stupid.
Third female singular	She	was not [wasn't)]	fat.
Third neutral singular	It	was not [wasn't]	barking.
Third (noun) singular	(noun)	was not [wasn't]	unhappy.
First plural	We	were not [weren't]	truthful.
Third plural	They	were not [weren't]	lying.
Third (nouns) plural	(nouns)	were not [weren't]	coming.

Person	Question Form	Adjective
First singular	Was I	driving?
Second singular	Were you	walking?
Third male singular	Was he	strong?
Third female singular	Was she	going?
Third neutral singular	Was it	digging?
Third (noun) singular	Was (noun)	sleeping?
First plural	Were we	funny?
Third plural	Were they	running?
Third (nouns) plural	Were (nouns)	sleepy?

PAST SIMPLE ACTIVE

Creation: In most cases this tense is used to describe single actions that have already happened:

did (optional)	**not** (if negative)	**base form of verb**

Examples: I did work at home *or* **She didn't enjoy** her meal

Note that **did** is normally used to add emphasis in positive statements and may be omitted (in which case the main verb carries the tense rather than the auxiliary verb), but it is always used in negative sentences. So first example sentence could be written as **I worked at home.** The past participle version of the verb is not needed in past simple - this would main apply to irregular verbs, such as went (past) and gone (past participle) rather than regular verbs whose past and past participles both end in *–ed.*

Example: I went to the market or **Sherry knew** how to do calculus.

Use this tense to describe the following:

Completed action in the past: use this tense to express the idea that an action started and finished at a specific time in the past and is now over. The time may or may not be specified.

Examples: I cooked my own dinner *or* Yesterday, **I saw** the new movie

A sequence of completed actions: it can be used to list a series of completed actions in the past.

Example: I went to the Post office, **bought** a stamp and **sent** the letter.

Longer action in the past: use with a longer action, usually indicated by a timescale, which starts and stops in the past.

Examples: I lived in the USA for two years before I moved here *or* You **were** on the phone for nearly an hour

Repetitive actions in the past: used to describe a habit or hobby which stopped in the past.

Examples: I used to smoke but **I gave** up *or* **I liked** skiing then **I got** too old.

Past facts: used to describe facts that are no longer true.

Examples: Oil **used** to be plentiful and cheap *or* When **I was** young, it **was** all green fields around here (note the use of the adverb clause with **when**).

Where time or place are mentioned: If the time when an event happened, or the place where it took place, are mentioned then use past simple.

Examples: I didn't go to bed until 11 p.m. *or* She **went** to the mall today.

WITH INTRANSITIVE VERBS

This tense uses the simple verb form as used with the various persons. Intransitive verbs do not need an object to form sentences; however, prepositional phrases plus either adverbs or 2nd prepositional phrases, can be added, as shown below. Note that (noun) means a singular noun; whereas, (nouns) means it is a plural noun.

Positive Form	Verb	Prepositional Phrases	
I	worked	in a university	at that moment.
You	went	to the library	in the morning.
He	studied	in the study room	in the afternoons.
She	cried	in her room	at night.
It	slept	in its kennel	with the other dog.
(Noun)	ran	in the park	near the river.
We	skied	in the snow	at the ski resort.
They	walked	on the path	next to the road.
(Nouns)	learned	about their subject	from their books.
Negative Form	Verb	Prepositional Phrases	
I did not	drive	across town	in the morning.
You did not	cycle	across the campus	on your bicycle.
He did not	doze	in a chair	near the heater.
She did not	eat	at the cafeteria	in her school.
It did not	bark	at strangers	near its home.
(noun) did not	reach	across the table	for the salt.
We did not	climb	up the hills	in the national park.
They did not	look	at their books	in the morning.
(nouns) did not	serve	in the shop	after school.
Question Form	Verb	Prepositional Phrases	
Did I	eat	at your house	in the evening?
Did you	come	past my house	in the morning?
Did he	write	up his notes	after his class?
Did she	play	on her computer	at night?
Did it	chew	on a bone	in its kennel?
Did (noun)	walk	under a bridge	on his way home?
Did we	go	to the party	in the evening?
Did they	fly	on their holiday	on the 17th?
Did (nouns)	look	at their iPads	under their desks?

WITH TRANSITIVE VERBS

This tense uses the simple verb form as used with the various persons. Transitive verbs need an object in order to form meaningful sentences, so noun phrases, plus optional prepositional phrases, can be added, as shown below. Note that (noun) means a singular noun; whereas, (nouns) means it is a plural noun.

Positive Form	Verb	Noun phrase	Prepositional
I	bought	the newspaper	at the local shop.
You	saw	the reports	from your boss.
He	ate	some noodles	at lunchtime.
She	sold	life insurance	from her office.
It	noticed	the people	in the park.
(Noun)	rode	the bus	to the office.
We	took	the same route	in the morning.
They	spent	their evenings	in the coffee shop.
(Nouns)	studied	the subject	in their books.
Negative Form	Verb	Noun phrase	Prepositional
I did not	do	the crossword	in the morning.
You did not	know	the answer	to my question.
He did not	bring	people	to the meeting.
She did not	love	her own body	in the past.
It did not	like	the food	in its bowl.
(noun) did not	teach	the students	on Friday.
We did not	buy	French fries	at any time.
They did not	catch	the bus	in the morning.
(nouns) did not	attend	the meetings	in the office.
Question Form	Verb	Noun phrase	Prepositional
Did I	have	the attention	of my class?
Did you	take	a shower	in the mornings?
Did he	write	his notes	during his class?
Did she	play	the cello	in the orchestra?
Did it	dig	holes	in the garden?
Did (noun)	watch	movies	after work?
Did we	attend	the party	at the club?
Did they	drive	their car	on the footpath?
Did (nouns)	find	the hidden posts	on the website?

PAST SIMPLE

Positive Form
I
You
He
She
It
(Noun)
We
They
(Nouns)

Negative Form
I did not
You did not
He did not
She did not
It did not
(noun) did not
We did not
They did not
(Nouns) did not

Question Form
Did I
Did you
Did he
Did she
Did it
Did (noun)
Did we
Did they
Did (nouns)

FUTURE SIMPLE USING BE

Creation: This is the simplest of tenses and is mainly used to describe the state the subject will be in by using an adjective or provides a last link between the subject and the object (usually a noun).

modal	not (if negative)	be

Examples:

I **will be** hot (state verb with adjective)

She **will not be** hot (negative state verb with adjective)

I **will be** the teacher (verb showing the link between the subject and object - in this case they are the same thing)

She **will not be** the teacher (negative verb proving that there will be NO link between the subject and the object).

We **will be** happy (positive verb linked to our emotional state).

They **will not be** happy (negative verb showing that will be no link to the their desired emotional state).

Use this tense to describe the following:

To describe a mental, emotional or physical state that is expected to be true. Note, this describes the state of the subject using an adjective.

Examples:

She **will be** indecisive.   (Mental state)
He **will be** sad.   (Emotional state)
They **will be** exhausted.   (Physical state)

To categorically state facts that are likely to be true in future: To confirm that something will be either true or untrue. You can use different modals to introduce doubt (see example 2).

Examples:

The world's population **will be** 9.7 billion in 2050.
The UK **may not be** in the EU in 2025. (Possibility using **may**)

State the likely future position of something in time or space. This construct uses '**be**' as an intransitive verb together with a <u>prepositional phrase</u> to determine a previous position.

Examples:

The car **will be** <u>in the garage</u>. (Position in place)
He **may not be** <u>on time</u>. (Possible position in time).

FUTURE SIMPLE USING BE

This tense uses the simple verb 'be' as used with the various persons. In order to form meaningful sentences adjectives are usually added, as shown below. Note that (noun) means a singular subject noun; whereas, (nouns) means it is a plural noun. Abbreviations are in brackets [ ].

Person	Positive Form		Adjective
	Subject	Verb	
First singular	I	will be	happy.
Second singular	You	will be	sad.
Third male singular	He	will be	clever.
Third female singular	She	will be	beautiful.
Third neutral singular	It	will be	smelly.
Third (noun) singular	(Noun)	will be	intelligent.
First plural	We	will be	angry.
Third plural	They	will be	cold.
Third (nouns) plural	(Nouns)	will be	Late.
Person	**Negative Form**		**Adjective**
First singular	I	will not [won't] be	listening.
Second singular	You	will not [won't] be	tall.
Third male singular	He	will not [won't] be	stupid.
Third female singular	She	will not [won't] be	fat.
Third neutral singular	It	will not [won't] be	barking.
Third (noun) singular	(noun)	will not [won't] be	unhappy.
First plural	We	will not [won't] be	truthful.
Third plural	They	will not [won't] be	lying.
Third (nouns) plural	(nouns)	will not [won't] be	coming.
Person	**Question Form**		**Adjective**
First singular		will I be	driving?
Second singular		will you be	walking?
Third male singular		will he be	strong?
Third female singular		will she be	going?
Third neutral singular		will it be	digging?
Third (noun) singular		will (noun) be	sleeping?
First plural		will we be	funny?
Third plural		will they be	running?
Third (nouns) plural		will (nouns) be	sleepy?

FUTURE SIMPLE ACTIVE

Creation: In most cases this tense is used to describe single future, pre planned or desired actions.

will (modal)	not (if negative)	base form of verb

Examples: I **will go** to the shops later *or* **She will not eat** anything spicy.

When used informally, **I will** can be contracted to **I'll** so the first example sentence would be **I'll go to the shops later. Will not** can be contracted to **won't** so the second sentence would be **She won't eat anything spicy.**

Use this tense to describe

Expressing a voluntary action: use this tense (with the word **will**) to describe an action you will undertake in the future. It can also be used to express a promise.

Examples: I **will read** the email and get back to you *or* **I'll see** you later.

Immediate action: use this tense to supply details of an action that will be started straight away. Note that the first example sentence is formal (business) and the second is informal.

Examples: Please hold and **I will put** you through *or* Hang on a second, **I'll find** a pen.

Pre-planned events: this tense may be used to talk about future actions that have been decided at the instant of speaking. In this case the sentence will start with the verbs **think**.

Example: I **think I'll have** another piece of cake.

Expressing a desire not to do something: use when wanting to say that an unplanned action will not be taking place, usually while giving a <u>reason</u>. It uses the negative form of the auxiliary verb **do.**

Example: I **don't think I'll go** to the shops today <u>as it's raining</u>.

Give details of a planned course of action: this tense can be used (together with the verb **be**) to outline the details of a plan. You can use an <u>infinitive</u> to state the intended action.

Example: She **will be** in work later *or* He **is intending** <u>to study</u> today

Make a prediction about the future: use with **be** to make a prediction about a future course of events.

<u>**Example:**</u> Managing the earth's resources **will be** crucial in the future.

WITH INTRANSITIVE VERBS

This tense uses the simple verb form as used with the various persons. Transitive verbs need an object in order to form meaningful sentences, so noun phrases, plus optional prepositional phrases, can be added, as shown below. Note that the modal verb 'will' has been used to form the future tense, other modals could be used instead to provide a different emphasis or mood.

Positive Form		Noun Phrase	Prepositional Phrase
I will (I'll)	buy	the newspaper	at the local shop.
You will (you'll)	see	the reports	from your boss.
He will (he'll)	eat	some noodles	at lunchtime.
She will (she'll)	sell	life insurance	from her office.
It will (it'll)	notice	the people	in the park.
(Noun) will ('ll)	ride	the bus	to the office.
We will (we'll)	take	the same route	in the morning.
They will (they'll)	spend	their evenings	in the coffee shop.
(Nouns) will ('ll)	study	the subject	in their books.
Negative Form		Noun Phrase	Prepositional Phrase
I will not (won't)	do	the crossword	in the morning.
You will not (won't)	know	the answer	to my question.
He will not (won't)	bring	people	to the meeting.
She will not (won't)	love	her own body	in the future.
It will not (won't)	like	the food	in its bowl.
(noun) will not (won't)	teach	the students	on Friday.
We will not (won't)	buy	French fries	at any time.
They will not (won't)	catch	the bus	in the morning.
(nouns) will not (won't)	attend	the meetings	in the office.
Question Form		Noun Phrase	Prepositional Phrase
Will I	have	the attention	of my class?
Will you	take	a shower	in the mornings?
Will he	write	his notes	during his class?
Will she	play	the cello	in the orchestra?
Will it	dig	holes	in the garden?
Will (noun)	watch	movies	after work?
Will we	attend	the party	at the club?
Will they	drive	their car	on the footpath?
Will (nouns)	find	the hidden posts	on the website?

WITH TRANSITIVE VERBS

This tense uses the simple verb form as used with the various persons. Transitive verbs need an object in order to form meaningful sentences, so noun phrases, plus optional prepositional phrases, can be added, as shown below. Note that the modal verb 'will' has been used to form the future tense, other modals could be used instead to provide a different emphasis or mood.

Positive Form		Noun Phrase	Prepositional Phrase
I will (I'll)	buy	the newspaper	at the local shop.
You will (you'll)	see	the reports	from your boss.
He will (he'll)	eat	some noodles	at lunchtime.
She will (she'll)	sell	life insurance	from her office.
It will (it'll)	notice	the people	in the park.
(Noun) will ('ll)	ride	the bus	to the office.
We will (we'll)	take	the same route	in the morning.
They will (they'll)	spend	their evenings	in the coffee shop.
(Nouns) will ('ll)	study	the subject	in their books.
Negative Form		Noun Phrase	Prepositional Phrase
I will not (won't)	do	the crossword	in the morning.
You will not (won't)	know	the answer	to my question.
He will not (won't)	bring	people	to the meeting.
She will not (won't)	love	her own body	in the future.
It will not (won't)	like	the food	in its bowl.
(noun) will not (won't)	teach	the students	on Friday.
We will not (won't)	buy	French fries	at any time.
They will not (won't)	catch	the bus	in the morning.
(nouns) will not (won't)	attend	the meetings	in the office.
Question Form		Noun Phrase	Prepositional Phrase
Will I	have	the attention	of my class?
Will you	take	a shower	in the mornings?
Will he	write	his notes	during his class?
Will she	play	the cello	in the orchestra?
Will it	dig	holes	in the garden?
Will (noun)	watch	movies	after work?
Will we	attend	the party	at the club?
Will they	drive	their car	on the footpath?
Will (nouns)	find	the hidden posts	on the website?

FUTURE SIMPLE

Positive Form
I'll
You'll
He'll
She'll
It'll
(Noun) 'll
We'll
They'll
(Noun) 'll

Negative Form
I won't
You won't
He won't
She won't
It won't
(Noun) won't
We won't
They won't
(Noun) won't

Question Form
Will I
Will you
Will he
Will she
Will it
Will (noun)
Will we
Will they
Will (noun)

CONTINUOUS TENSE

The construction of verb tenses, other than simple tenses, can appear to be quite confusing when you first study the English language. The use of auxiliary verbs adds an extra layer of complexity to the process. However, when you actually look at the construction of the various tenses you will see that they are actually very straightforward.

Forming the continuous tense using BE

We can start by looking at the use of the simple tense using the various forms of the verb 'be'. This verb can, and usually does, take an adjective as its object rather than a noun and is used to say how we are, in terms of our physical state (I am **hot**), our emotional state (I am **sad**), the characteristics of something (it was **fun**) or our mental state (I am **clever**). We can also use adjectives that are based upon actions, known as present participles (with an 'ing' attached to the end of the verb), to describe something that is affecting us in some way, such as physically (for **Example: running** or **walking**), mentally (for **Example: thinking** or **studying**) or emotionally (for example **crying** or **laughing**). These statements can be used to answer the question "**what are you doing?**" So, for example, you can describe the states of being, using the simple tense, for various persons, with a suitable form of 'be', like so:

I am running	describing my physical state
You are thinking	describing your mental state
She is crying	describing her emotional state
This is exciting	describing an effect (aka personal observation or characteristic)

We can add prepositional, or noun, phrases to these explanations of our state, to say what it is that is affecting us or what is being affected by our state. In the examples, the <u>prepositional</u> phrases are in bold.

I am running **<u>around</u> the track.**	(answers what)
You are thinking **<u>about</u> your girlfriend.**	(answers who)
She is crying **<u>because of</u> the sad movie.**	(answers why)

These phrases are regarded as the objects of the verb + adjective. Once an object has been added they go from being the simple tense to something else.

This construct, of the verb 'be' followed by a descriptive adjective, is known as the **continuous tense**. The following pages give examples of the various forms of continuous tense for each person, in the positive, negative and question forms, plus exercises for you to create your own.

Be is the most important and also the most irregular verb in English It may be used as an auxiliary [A], an intransitive [I] or a linking [L] verb. It is composed of a number of verbs, from old English, that have been merged together (hence the irregularity). The verbs that were merged were **be, become, come into existence, grow** and **happen.**

The verb Be has eight different forms in English

Form	Uses and pronunciation	
Be	Used in future tense forms (e.g. will be)	biː
Am	1st person singular, present tense	æm
Are	2nd person singular, 1st and 3rd person plural	ɑːr
Is	3rd person singular present tense	ɪz
Was	1st and 3rd person singular, past tense	wɒz
Were	2nd person singular, 1st and 3rd person plural, past tense	wɜːr
Being	Present Participle version	biːɪŋ
Been	Past participle version	biːn

When it is used in the composition of verb structures it shows that the subject of the verb is in a state of being. For example in the sentence **I am singing**, the 'be' verb (**am**) is used to show that my present (physical) state is performing some action, in this case described by the present participle (adjectival) form of the main verb, **singing**. In the sentence **she is thinking**, it shows that the subject's current (mental) state is that she is thinking. This verb will, in continuous verb forms where it is used as an auxiliary verb, carry the tense. For example, he **was** singing (**past**), he **is** singing (**present**) and he **will be** singing (**future**).

When it is used in the continuous form (**being**) it means temporarily behaving in a particular way (quite often negative). For **Example:**

He is being rude means that at this moment in time he is exhibiting rudeness but not always.

He is rude, on the other hand, means that it is his usual state, so he is <u>always</u> rude.

PRESENT CONTINUOUS ACTIVE

Creation: This tense is used to describe actions currently in progress. It takes the form

be (verb)	not (optional)	present participle

Examples: I am working today *or* **They are watching** TV *or* **Sheila is not walking** the dog

Note that present participle (adjective) forms of the verb have '*ing*' appended, so '**walk**' becomes '**walking**'

Questions are formed by reversing the subject/auxiliary verb order.

Example: Are you working today?

Use this tense to describe the following:

Now: Use to express the idea that something is happening now, at this very moment. It can also be used to show that something is not happening.

Examples: What **are** you **doing** now? *or* I **am not telling** you again

Actions in progress that may not be imminently completed: used to describe being in the process of doing a longer action which is in progress; however, it might not be being done at this exact moment in time.

Examples: I am studying English *or* I **am not going** out with Liz any more

Near future: use to indicate that something has been planned to happen in the near future. Note that the emphasis is on the fact that the event was already planned prior to talking about it.

Examples: I am marking exams tonight *or* **Are** you **coming** to the party tomorrow? Yes, **I'm coming.** (Note the intransitive use of the verb and the abbreviation of '**am**')

Non habitual actions happening around now: use when the actions are happening around the present time and are not permanent.

Example: Peter **is** <u>currently</u> **living** in the student dormitories.

Multiple actions happening around now: use to describe two or more actions happening around now. If one action is less important then that action would be used in simple tense (see the 2nd example).

Examples: Stella **is cooking** the food while Bill **is laying** the table
Stella **is cooking** the food while Bill **lays** the table.

WITH INTRANSITIVE VERBS

This tense uses the state verb be, with the various persons, with the contracted forms (used in speech) in parentheses. This verb is followed by present participle adjectives. In order to form meaningful sentences, prepositional phrases can be added, as shown below.

Positive Form	Adjective	Prepositional Phrase
I am (I'm)	working	on my project.
You are (you're)	going	to my house.
He is (he's)	studying	in his room.
She is (she's)	crying	at the sad movie.
It is (it's)	sleeping	in its kennel.
(Noun) is ('s)	running	around the track.
We are (we're)	skiing	through the snow.
They are (they're)	walking	to their classroom.
(Nouns) are	reading	for their thesis.
Negative Form	Adjective	Prepositional Phrase
I am not (I'm not)	driving	to the party.
You are not (You're not)	cycling	across the campus.
He is not (He isn't)	dozing	in a chair.
She is not (She isn't)	eating	in the restaurant.
It is not (It isn't)	barking	at the stranger.
(noun) is not (isn't)	reaching	for the salt.
We are not (We're not)	climbing	up the hill.
They are not (They're not)	looking	at the rainbow
(nouns) are not (aren't)	serving	at the shop.
Question Form	Adjective	Prepositional Phrase
Am I	eating	at your house?
Are you	coming	to my party?
Is he	writing	down the details?
Is she	reading	through her notes?
Is it	chewing	on a bone?
Is (noun)	walking	through the park?
Are we	going	on the bus?
Are they	flying	on the 7th?
Are (nouns)	looking	through their books

TRANSITIVE VERBS

This tense uses the state verb be, followed by present participle adjectives. In order to form sentences optional noun and prepositional phrases can be added, as shown below. Note that the adjectives that are shaded create abstract (state) verbs and they shouldn't be used in this tense (they should be used in the simple tense form instead using 'do' instead of 'be'). They have been left in to maintain the continuity.

Positive Form	Adjective	Noun & Prepositional Phrases	
I am (I'm)	buying	the newspaper	at the local shop.
You are (you're)	seeing	the reports	from your boss.
He is (he's)	eating	some noodles	at lunchtime.
She is (she's)	selling	life insurance	from her office.
It is (it's)	noticing	the people	in the park.
(Noun) is ('s)	riding	the bus	to the office.
We are (we're)	taking	the same route	in the morning.
They are (they're)	spending	their evenings	in the coffee shop.
(Nouns) are	studying	the subject	in their books.
Negative Form	Adjective	Noun & Prepositional Phrases	
I am not (I'm not)	doing	the crossword	in the morning.
You are not (You're not)	knowing	the answer	to my question.
He is not (He isn't)	bringing	people	to the meeting.
She is not (She isn't)	loving	her own body	at the moment.
It is not (It isn't)	liking	the food	in its bowl.
(noun) is not (isn't)	teaching	the students	on Friday.
We are not (We're not)	buying	French fries	at any time.
They are not (They're not)	catching	the bus	in the morning.
(nouns) are not (aren't)	attending	the meetings	in the office.
Question Form	Adjective	Noun & Prepositional Phrases	
Am I	having	the attention	of my class?
Are you	taking	a shower	in the mornings?
Is he	writing	his notes	during his class?
Is she	playing	the cello	in the orchestra?
Is it	digging	holes	in the garden?
Is (noun)	watching	movies	after work?
Are we	attending	the party	at the club?
Are they	driving	their car	on the footpath?
Are (nouns)	finding	the posts	on the web?

PRESENT CONTINUOUS

Positive Form

I am

You are

He is

She is

It is

(Noun) is

We are

They are

(nouns) are

Negative Form

I am not

You are not

He is not

She is not

It is not

(noun) is not

We are not

They are not

(nouns) are not

Question Form

Am I

Are you

Is he

Is she

Is it

Is (noun)

Are we

Are they

Are (nouns)

PAST CONTINUOUS ACTIVE

Creation: This tense is used to describe actions that were in progress at a particular point in the past. It takes the form:

be (past tense form)	**not** (optional)	**present participle**

Note that the action being described was started before the particular moment but has not yet finished at that moment. In other words whenever this tense is used then it is on the assumption that the listener knows what time is being talked about. Past tense conjunctions are **was** or **were**.

Use this tense to describe:

Interrupted action in the past is used to indicate that a longer action in the past was interrupted with the interruption usually being of a shorter duration. It can be a real interruption or just an interruption in time.

Examples: I **was having** a shower and the phone rang *or* The class **was staring** at the goat outside the window. (The goat interrupted my class).

Specific time as an interruption in addition to you can also use a specific time as an interruption. Note that the main difference between this tense and the simple past is that in the simple past, a specific time is used to show when an action began or finished; in this tense a specific time only briefly interrupts the action or states the action was still happening at a specific time. The time is defined using a *prepositional phrase.*

Examples: The class **was** still **going** a*t 6 p.m. or By midnight* I **was starting** to worry about her.

Simultaneous actions: use to express the idea that two or more actions were happening at the same time and in parallel. If both actions are not of equal importance then the least important uses simple tense.

Examples: I **was shopping** while she **was sleeping** *or* I **was studying** and **listening** to the radio *or* I **was working** while she **watched** the television.

Atmosphere: it can also be used to describe a series of parallel actions to describe the atmosphere at a particular time in the past.

Example: When I was young the trains **were running** on time, doors **were being** left unlocked and families **were taking** care of each other.

Annoyance using *always*: This tense is often used to express annoyance at constantly repeated actions. Note the adverb <u>always</u>.

Examples: The bus **was** <u>always</u> **arriving** late *or* She **was** <u>always</u> **saying** how beautiful she was.

WITH INTRANSITIVE VERBS

To form the past continuous forms we will use the same adjectives and prepositional phrases as we did in the present tense. The only difference being is that we are now using the past version of the verb 'be'. The adjectives (present participles) do not change because they are still being used in the same way - to describe a continuing state – but the 'be' verb needs to change to reflect that the action or state has finished already.

Negative Form	Adjective	Prepositional Phrase
I was	working	on my project.
You were	going	to my house.
He was	studying	in his room.
She was	crying	at the sad movie.
It was	sleeping	in its kennel.
(Noun) was	running	around the track.
We were	skiing	through the snow.
They were	walking	to their classroom.
(Nouns) were	reading	for their thesis.

Negative Form	Adjective	Prepositional Phrase
I was not (wasn't)	driving	to the party.
You were not (weren't)	cycling	across the campus.
He was not (wasn't)	dozing	in a chair.
She was not (wasn't)	eating	in the restaurant.
It was not (wasn't)	barking	at the stranger.
(noun) was not (wasn't)	reaching	for the salt.
We were not (weren't)	climbing	up the hill.
They were not (weren't)	looking	at the rainbow
(nouns) were not (weren't)	serving	at the shop.

Question Form	Adjective	Prepositional Phrase
Was I	eating	at your house?
Were you	coming	to my party?
Was he	writing	down the details?
Was she	reading	through her notes?
Was it	chewing	on a bone?
Was (noun)	walking	through the park?
Were we	going	on the bus?
Were they	flying	on the 7th?
Were (nouns)	looking	through their books?

WITH TRANSITIVE VERBS

To form the past continuous forms we will use the same adjectives, noun phrases and prepositional phrases as we did in the present tense. The only difference being is that we are now using the past version of the verb 'be'. The adjectives (present participles) do not change because they are still being used in the same way - to describe a continuing state – but the 'be' verb needs to change to reflect that the action or state has finished already.

Positive Form	Adjective	Noun & Prepositional Phrases	
I was	buying	the newspaper	at the local shop.
You were	seeing	the reports	from your boss.
He was	eating	some noodles	at lunchtime.
She was	selling	live insurance	from her office.
It was	noticing	the people	in the park.
(Noun) was	riding	the bus	to the office.
We were	taking	the same route	in the morning.
They were	spending	their evenings	in the coffee shop.
(Nouns) were	studying	the subject	in their books.
Negative Form	**Adjective**	**Noun & Prepositional Phrases**	
I was not (wasn't)	doing	the crossword	in the morning.
You were not (weren't)	knowing	the answer	to my question.
He was not (he wasn't)	bringing	people	to the meeting.
She was not (she wasn't)	loving	her own body	in the past.
It was not (it wasn't)	liking	the food	in its bowl.
(noun) was not (wasn't)	teaching	the students	on Friday.
We are not (weren't)	buying	French fries	at any time.
They were not (weren't)	catching	the bus	in the morning.
(nouns) are not (weren't)	attending	the meetings	in the office.
Positive Form	**Adjective**	**Noun & Prepositional Phrases**	
Was I	having	the attention	of my class?
Were you	taking	a shower	in the mornings?
Was he	writing	his notes	during his class?
Was she	playing	the cello	in the orchestra?
Was it	digging	holes	in the garden?
Was (noun)	watching	movies	after work?
Were we	attending	the party	at the club?
Were they	driving	their car	on the footpath?
Were (nouns)	finding	the posts	on the web?

PAST CONTINUOUS WORKSHEET

Positive Form

I was

You were

He was

She was

It was

(Noun) was

We were

They were

(Plural) were

Negative Form

I was not

You were not

He was not

She was not

It was not

(Noun) was not

We were not

They were not

(Plural) were not

Question Form

Was I

Were you

Was he

Was she

Was it

Was (noun)

Were we

Were they

Were (plural)

FUTURE CONTINUOUS ACTIVE

Creation: Used to describe actions that are likely to be in progress (but not finished) at a particular point in the future.

will (modal)	**not** (optional)	**be** (aux)	**present participle**

Examples: I **will not be watching** the movie tonight *or* She **will be catching** a flight to Beijing this evening.

Note in the first sentence **I will not** can be contracted to **I won't** and in the second sentence **she will** can be contracted to **she'll**. In formal English **shall** is often used instead of **will** when the subject is either I or We: **We shall** be going to the party at 9 p.m. It will have the same contraction as I will: **I will** and **I shall** both contract to **I'll**.

Use this tense to describe:

Future actions at a set time: use to say what will be happening at a fixed time in the future.

Example: I **will be playing** badminton at 6 p.m. *or* We **will be eating** at 7 p.m.

Interrupted action in the future: use this tense to indicate that a longer action in the future will be interrupted by a shorter action (either an action or a period of time) in the future.

Example: I **will be reading** a book when you arrive

Specifying a timed interruption in the future: this tense can also be used to express an interruption that will happen at a specific time rather than (as in the previous example) an action

Example: She **will be going** to the supermarket at 10 a.m. to do her shopping

Parallel actions in the future: you can also use this tense to describe two (or more) actions that are occurring simultaneously in the future

Example: Tonight, she **will be watching** the TV while her husband is out.

Predictions of social interaction in the future: this tense can be used to predict what sort of social interactions are likely to be happening at a future point in time, usually by describing parallel actions.

Example:

I think the class tonight **will be boring** because our normal teacher is away and many students will be absent.

WITH INTRANSITIVE VERBS

The difference between this tense and the present or past forms is that we use the simple (bare infinitive) version of the word 'be' plus a suitable modal verb. The most commonly used modal verb is 'will' so that is what we'll use here, to change the intent we can use a different modal verb in its place.

Positive Form	Adjective	Prepositional Phrase
I will be (I'll be)	working	on my project.
You will be (you'll be)	going	to my house.
He will be (you'll be)	studying	in his room.
She will be (she'll be)	crying	at the sad movie.
It will be (it'll be)	sleeping	in its kennel.
(Noun) will be ('ll be)	running	around the track.
We will be (we'll be)	skiing	through the snow.
They will be (they'll be)	walking	to their classroom.
(Nouns) will be ('ll be)	reading	for their thesis.
Negative Form	Adjective	Prepositional Phrase
I will not be (I won't be)	driving	to the party.
You will not be (you won't be)	cycling	across the campus.
He will not be (he won't be)	dozing	in a chair.
She will not be (she won't be)	eating	in the restaurant.
It will not be (it won't be)	barking	at the stranger.
(noun) will not be (won't be)	reaching	for the salt.
We will not be (we won't be)	climbing	up the hill.
They will not be (they won't be)	looking	at the rainbow
(nouns) will not be (won't be)	serving	at the shop.
Question Form	Adjective	Prepositional Phrase
Will I be	eating	at your house?
Will you be	coming	to my party?
Will he be	writing	down the details?
Will she be	reading	through her notes?
Will it be	chewing	on a bone?
Will (noun) be	walking	through the park?
Will we be	going	on the bus?
Will they be	flying	on the 7th?
Will (nouns) be	looking	through their books?

FUTURE CONTINUOUS TENSE

The difference between this tense and the present or past forms is that we use the simple (bare infinitive) version of the word 'be' plus a suitable modal verb. The most commonly used modal verb is 'will' so that is what we'll use here, to change the intent we can use a different modal verb in its place. Note that the adjectives that are shaded create abstract (state) verbs and they shouldn't be used in this tense (use the simple tense instead).

Positive Form	Adjective	Noun & Prepositional Phrases	
I will be (I'll be)	buying	the newspaper	at the local shop.
You will be (you'll be)	seeing	the reports	from your boss.
He will be (you'll be)	eating	some noodles	at lunchtime.
She will be (she'll be)	selling	life insurance	from her office.
It will be (it'll be)	noticing	the people	in the park.
(Noun) will be ('ll be)	riding	the bus	to the office.
We will be (we'll be)	taking	the same route	in the morning.
They will be (they'll be)	spending	their evenings	in the coffee shop.
(Nouns) will be ('ll be)	studying	the subject	in their books.
Positive Form	Adjective	Noun & Prepositional Phrases	
I will not (won't) be	doing	the crossword	in the morning.
You will not (won't) be	knowing	the answer	to my question.
He will not (won't) be	bringing	people	to the meeting.
She will not be (won't) be	loving	her own body	in the future.
It will not (won't) be	liking	the food	in its bowl.
(noun) will not (won't) be	teaching	the students	on Friday.
We will not (won't) be	buying	French fries	at any time.
They will not (won't) be)	catching	the bus	in the morning.
(nouns) will not (won't be)	attending	the meetings	in the office.
Positive Form	Adjective	Noun & Prepositional Phrases	
Will I be	having	the attention	of my class?
Will you be	taking	a shower	in the mornings?
Will he be	writing	his notes	during his class?
Will she be	playing	the cello	in the orchestra?
Will it be	digging	holes	in the garden?
Will (noun) be	watching	movies	after work?
Will we be	attending	the party	at the club?
Will they be	driving	their car	on the footpath?
Will (nouns) be	finding	the posts	on the website?

FUTURE CONTINUOUS

I'll be
You'll be
He'll be
She'll be
It'll be
(Noun) 'll be
We'll be
They'll be
(Nouns) 'll be

I won't be
You won't be
He won't be
She won't be
It won't be
(noun) won't be
We won't be
They won't be
(nouns) won't be

Will I be
Will you be
Will he be
Will she be
Will it be
Will (noun) be
Will we be
Will they be
Will (nouns) be

Verb Tenses

PERFECT TENSE

Have is the second most important verb in English. It is an irregular verb with the following structures: have, has, had, and having. It originally came from the Old Saxon word 'hebbjan' meaning 'to grasp' and has a number of meanings, which are; to be subject to something, to undergo an experience or to achieve or possess something. For **Example:**

Meaning	Example Sentence	Tense
To be subject to	I **have** been ordered to go on duty.	Perfect
To undergo an experience	I **have** seen a solar eclipse.	Perfect
To achieve something	I **have** passed my exam.	Perfect
To possess something	I **have** a new car.	Simple

It has also been used as a modal verb (in the form **'have to'**) since the late 1500s, where it is used in a similar way to must (**have to** now tends to mean that an action is imposed by others – I **have to** be at work by 8 am – whereas **must** tends to mean that the obligation to do something is imposed upon oneself – I **must** go on a diet). Note that in this form it is generally not regarded as a true modal by grammarians (even though it is commonly used as such) because it can carry the tense (I **had** to go, I **have** to go, she **has** to go) and so the following verb is in its infinitive form. Indeed, if you study the structure then you will see that it serves to allow the subject to possess, own, do the action, or exist in the state described by the subsequent infinitive.

The most common use is to form perfect tenses. It can be used more than once on the verb structure. For example, study the following sentence: She **has to have had** plastic surgery. The **'has to'** is used to indicate that something most probably happened, the **'have'** means that the subject has experience of, is subject to, or owns, something and the **'had'** indicates that the subject was subject to something in the past and it is effecting the present.

Finally, it forms the root of a number of other verbs such as behave (act in an approved way) and shave (to cut). The negative versions of the verb are have not (haven't), had not (hadn't) and has not (hasn't). It is abbreviated in speech, when used in perfect tense forms, as I've (I have), he's (he has) and she'd (she had): note that the abbreviated 3rd person singular form is the same (he's) as the 3rd person singular of the verb 'be'; he is (he's).

PERFECT TENSE FORMATION

When we studied the continuous tense we saw how an adjective ending in '**ing**', also known as a present participle, is used to describe the characteristics of something or someone. Another type of adjective, is one that ends in '**ed**', which is also known as a past participle. This type of adjective describes a feeling rather than the effect (characteristic). We can see how they are used by studying the following sentences:

He is boring   describes the effect he has on others (observed characteristic).
He is bored   describes how he feels (based on personal feelings).

Note, they are both formed from verbs and both are used in verb phrase formations. Verb phrases are a sequence of words that form what we know as a tense – so, in the sentence, **I am feeling** happy, '**am feeling** ', is the verb phrase (verb + adjective formed from a verb).

In the previous sub-section, on the formation of the continuous tense, we saw how the auxiliary verb '**be**' is used is used to describe the state and, together with the characteristic adjective, form the continuous tense. However, what about if we want to describe a possession instead of a state? The obvious word to use in this instance is the verb '**have**', for example, **I have a car** or **She has a dog.** If we use this verb with an '**ed**' adjective then we can describe the possession of an achievement (**I have passed** my exams), a thing (**I have got** a car), an experience (**I have been** to Krabi) or a result (**I have finished** my work). This verb form is called the **perfect tense**.

As with any possession you either obtained it sometime in the past and still have it (present tense), you got in sometime in the past but you've now lost it (past tense) or you believe you will get it at some point in the future, but you haven't got it yet (future tense). It doesn't matter when you had (past), have (present) or will have it (future); the possession of it is the important thing. So, unlike the continuous tense, which has a set time period (as you cannot be in a state forever [except dead!]), there is usually no need for a time period with this tense; although you could add one if you choose – I <u>have had</u> a dog for two years. The future perfect tense may have a prepositional phrase or an adverbial clause appended to it, to indicate when the acquisition is going to take place – I will have arrived in Bangkok <u>by tomorrow</u> (prepositional phrase) or I will have already seen the pyramids <u>when you arrive</u> (adverbial clause). The future tense form, together with a suitable modal verb, can be used to discuss events that happened in the past that are affecting the present and the past tense forms can be used to create conditional sentences.

PRESENT PERFECT ACTIVE

Creation: This tense is used to describe current actions with an emphasis on the result rather than when it happened. It takes the form:

have/has (optional)	**not** (if negative)	**past participle**

Examples: I have seen Vesuvius *or* **Sally has not been** to Italy.

Note that the auxiliary verb (**have**) becomes **has** when the subject is 3rd person singular (He, She, It, Name), however the main verb does not change. Americans often use past simple rather than present perfect.

Use this tense to describe the following:

Experience: Use the Present Perfect to describe an experience you had or one that you have never had. The Present Perfect is NOT used to describe a specific event.

Example: I have been to Bangkok once *or* She **hasn't read** my letter yet.

Changes over a period of time: Use the Present Perfect to talk about a change that has happened over a period of time.

Example: Bangkok **has become** more crowded in the last ten years.

Accomplishments: Use the Present Perfect to list the accomplishments of people without giving a specific time.

Example: Bangkok **has built** a Skytrain network to ease traffic congestion.

Something you are expecting to happen: use the Present Perfect to say that an action which was expected to happen but still hasn't happened.

Example: The students **haven't finished** their essays yet.

Multiple actions that have happened at different times: use the Present Perfect to talk about several different actions which have occurred in the past at different times. It can be used to suggest that the process is not complete and more actions are possible.

Example: They **have had** a lot of problems to overcome in this project.

Continuing situations: It can be used with the prepositions **since** and **for** to indicate actions that have continued over a period of time (see present perfect continuous to provide the length of time).

Examples: I have lived in Bangkok **since** 2007

Expressing Regret: It can be used with the modal **should** to express regret.

Example: I should have listened to my father's advice when I was a child.

WITH INTRANSITIVE VERBS

This verb form uses the past participle adjectives and the present tense version of the verb 'have' to form the tense. In the examples, prepositional phrases have been used to form sentences.

Positive Form	Adjective	Prepositional Phrase
I have (I've)	worked	on my project.
You have (you've)	gone	to my house.
He has (he's)	studied	in his room.
She has (she's)	cried	at the sad movie.
It has (it's)	slept	in its kennel.
(noun) has ('s)	run	around the track.
We have (we've)	skied	through the snow.
They have (they've)	walked	to their classroom.
(nouns) have ('ve)	read	for their thesis.
Negative Form	**Adjective**	**Prepositional Phrase**
I have not (haven't)	driven	to the party.
You have not (haven't)	cycled	across the campus.
He has not (hasn't)	dozed	in a chair.
She has not (hasn't)	eaten	in the restaurant.
It has not (hasn't)	barked	at the stranger.
(noun) has not (hasn't)	reached	for the salt.
We have not (haven't)	climbed	up the hill.
They have not (haven't)	looked	at the rainbow
(nouns) have not (haven't)	served	at the shop.
Question Form	**Adjective**	**Prepositional Phrase**
Have I	eaten	at your house?
Have you	come	to my party?
Has he	written	down the details?
Has she	read	through her notes?
Has it	chewed	on a bone?
Has (noun)	walked	through the park?
Have we	gone	on the bus?
Have they	flown	on the 7th?
Have (nouns)	looked	through their books?

Verb Tenses

WITH TRANSITIVE VERBS

This verb form uses the past participle adjectives and the present tense version of the verb 'have' to form the tense. In the examples, noun phrases have been used to form sentences. Prepositional phrases can be added after the noun phrases.

Positive Form	Adjective	Noun Phrase
I have (I've)	bought	the newspaper
You have (you've)	seen	the reports
He has (he's)	eaten	some noodles
She has (she's)	sold	insurance
It has (it's)	noticed	the people
(noun) has ('s)	ridden	the bus
We have (we've)	taken	the same route
They have (they've)	spent	their evenings
(nouns) have ('ve)	studied	the subject
Negative Form	Adjective	Noun Phrase
I have not (haven't)	done	the crossword
You have not (haven't)	known	the answer
He has not (hasn't)	brought	people
She has not (hasn't)	loved	her own body
It has not (hasn't)	liked	the food
(noun) has not (hasn't)	taught	the students
We have not (haven't)	bought	French fries
They have not (haven't)	caught	the bus
(nouns) have not (haven't)	attended	the meetings
Question Form	Adjective	Noun Phrase
Have I	had	the attention
Have you	taken	a shower
Has he	written	his notes
Has she	played	the cello
Has it	dug	holes
Has (noun)	watched	movies
Have we	attended	the party
Have they	driven	their car
Have (nouns)	found	the hidden posts

PRESENT PERFECT WORKSHEET

Positive Form

I have
You have
He has
She has
It has
        has
We have
They have
        have

Negative Form

I have not
You have not
He has not
She has not
It has not
        has not
We have not
They have not
        have not

Question Form

Have I
Have you
Has he
Has she
Has it
Has
Have we
Have they
Have

PAST PERFECT ACTIVE

Creation: This tense is used to describe an action in the past that took place before another action in the past. It takes the form:

had (verb)	not (if negative)	past participle

Examples: He **had not arrived** when I got there *or* She **had finished** eating before I arrived.

Note that **had not** is usually contracted into **hadn't** when using this tense. So the first sentence would normally be phrased as He **hadn't arrived** when I got there, with '**had not**' used in speech for emphasis.

Use this tense to describe:

Completed action before another action in the past: used to show that something happened before a specific time or action in the past.

Examples: I **had** never **realised** how beautiful Thailand was until I went there *or* I **had studied** German before I started studying English

Specific Times with the Past Perfect: this tense can be used, unlike with the Present Perfect, to express a specific time. But it is optional in that if the words **before** or **after** are used in the sentence then it becomes past simple.

Examples: She **had completed** her degree in 1994 *or* England **had** last **won** the world cup in 1966

Reason for a past action: used for supplying a reason for course of action undertaken in the past.

Example: I needed a rest as I **had worked** since early in the morning.

Reported speech: Past perfect is often used in reported speech after the verbs **asked, explained, said, told, thought** *or* **wondered** had already been used in the sentence. For **Example:**

He **asked** his friend what **had happened** the previous night.
The management **explained** why they **had closed** the plant.
Ted **said** he **had finished** the report already.
We **told** them that they **had arrived** too late.
She **thought** she **had seen** him before.
I **wondered** if they **had watched** my video.

Lack of something: This tense can be used to express a lack of something rather than a specific action.

Examples: He **had <u>never</u> seen** a Skyscraper until he visited New York or With only 20% of the votes the government **had lacked** a mandate.

WITH INTRANSITIVE VERBS

This verb form uses the past participle adjectives and the past tense version of the verb 'have' to form the tense. You can use this verb tense to create conditional statements (If you **had listened** to me it wouldn't have happened *or* **Had** you **been** careful you wouldn't have crashed).

Positive Form	Adjective	Prepositional Phrase
I had (I'd)	worked	on my project.
You had (you'd)	gone	to my house.
He had (he'd)	studied	in his room.
She had (she'd)	cried	at the sad movie.
It had (it'd)	slept	in its kennel.
(noun) had ('d)	run	around the track.
We had (we'd)	skied	through the snow.
They had (they'd)	walked	to their classroom.
(nouns) have ('d)	read	for their thesis.
Negative Form	**Adjective**	**Prepositional Phrase**
I had not (hadn't)	driven	to the party.
You had not (hadn't)	cycled	across the campus.
He had not (hadn't)	dozed	in a chair.
She had not (hadn't)	eaten	in the restaurant.
It had not (hadn't)	barked	at the stranger.
(noun) had not (hadn't)	reached	for the salt.
We had not (hadn't)	climbed	up the hill.
They had not (hadn't)	looked	at the rainbow
(nouns) had not (hadn't)	served	at the shop.
Question Form	**Adjective**	**Prepositional Phrase**
Had I	eaten	at your house?
Had you	come	to my party?
Had he	written	down the details?
Had she	read	through her notes?
Had it	chewed	on a bone?
Had (noun)	walked	through the park?
Had we	gone	on the bus?
Had they	flown	on the 7th?
Had (nouns)	looked	through their books?

WITH TRANSITIVE VERBS

This verb form uses the past participle adjectives and the past tense version of the verb 'have' to form the tense. As they are transitive verbs they need an object and, in most cases, they would use an additional adverb or prepositional phrase to state the condition.

Positive Form	Adjective	Noun Phrase
I had (I'd)	bought	the newspaper
You had (you'd)	seen	the reports
He had (he'd)	eaten	some noodles
She had (she'd)	sold	insurance
It had (it'd)	noticed	the people
(noun) had ('d)	ridden	the bus
We had (we'd)	taken	the same route
They had (they'd)	spent	their evenings
(nouns) have ('d)	studied	the subject
Negative Form	Adjective	Noun Phrase
I had not (hadn't)	done	the crossword
You had not (hadn't)	known	the answer
He had not (hadn't)	brought	people
She had not (hadn't)	loved	her own body
It had not (hadn't)	liked	the food
(noun) had not (hadn't)	taught	the students
We had not (hadn't)	bought	French fries
They had not (hadn't)	caught	the bus
(nouns) had not (hadn't)	attended	the meetings
Question Form	Adjective	Noun Phrase
Had I	had	the attention
Had you	taken	a shower
Had he	written	his notes
Had she	played	the cello
Had it	dug	holes
Had (noun)	watched	movies
Had we	attended	the party
Had they	driven	their car
Had (nouns)	found	the hidden posts

PAST PERFECT WORKSHEET

Positive Form

I had
You had
He had
She had
It had
      had
We had
They had
      have

Negative Form

I had not
You had not
He had not
She had not
It had not
      had not
We had not
They had not
      had not

Question Form

Had I
Had you
Had he
Had she
Had it
Had
Had we
Had they
Had

FUTURE PERFECT ACTIVE

Creation: In most cases this tense is used to describe current or repeated actions. It takes the form:

will (modal)	**not** (if negative)	**have** (aux)	**past participle**

Examples: I will not have finished by the time she gets here *or* **She will have brought** cookies.

Most modal verbs can be used with this tense to express different intent or feelings so you can use the modal to describe something that happened in the past that is affecting the present or the future. For **Example:**

We **will have** completed the project by this evening. *(definite action)*
You **have to** have permission to enter. *(action by others needed first)*
I **must** have dropped it somewhere. *(stating a logical explanation)*
You **need to** have filled out this form. *(stating a requirement)*
We **shall** have eaten by 6 *(prediction of a definite event for 1st persons)*
Can you have taken a sample by tonight? *(stating a possibility)*
I **ought to** have passed. *(something should have happened but didn't)*
You **should** have studied harder. *(preferred action that didn't happen)*
I **would** have gone, but I was watching the football. *(reason for inaction)*
I **may** have got what you need. *(stating a 50% possibility)*
I **might** have gone bald by washing my hair. *(unlikely possibility)*
I **could** have told you that would happen. *(action that would have helped)*

Use this tense to describe:

Completed action before a time in the future: use this tense to describe an action that will happen before a time in the future

Examples: He **will have become** a millionaire by the time he reaches 30 *or* she **won't have finished** her work by tonight.

Completed action before another action in the future: use this tense to describe an action that will happen before another action in the future.

Example: We **will have taken** steps, before the CEO gets here, to ensure it won't happen again.

Duration before some action happening in the future:

Examples: It **will have taken** at least two hours to fix my computer *or* By the 6th of next month we **will have visited** Bangkok.

WITH INTRANSITIVE VERBS

This verb form uses the past participle adjectives and the past tense version of the verb 'have' to form the tense. As these verbs are intransitive the sentences can use a prepositional phrase to add further details.

Positive Form	Adjective	Prepositional Phrase
I will have (I'll have)	worked	on my project.
You will have (you'll have)	gone	to my house.
He will have (he'll have)	studied	in his room.
She will have (she'll have)	cried	at the sad movie.
It will have (it'll have)	slept	in its kennel.
(noun) will have ('ll have)	run	around the track.
We will have (we'll have)	skied	through the snow.
They will have (they'll have)	walked	to their classroom.
(nouns) have ('ll have)	read	for their thesis.

Negative Form	Adjective	Prepositional Phrase
I will not (won't) have	driven	to the party.
You will not (won't) have	cycled	across the campus.
He will not (won't) have	dozed	in a chair.
She will not (won't) have	eaten	in the restaurant.
It will not (won't) have	barked	at the stranger.
(noun) will not (won't) have	reached	for the salt.
We will not (won't) have	climbed	up the hill.
They will not (won't) have	looked	at the rainbow
(nouns) will not (won't) have	served	at the shop.

Question Form	Adjective	Prepositional Phrase
Will I have	eaten	at your house?
Will you have	come	to my party?
Will he have	written	down the details?
Will she have	read	through her notes?
Will it have	chewed	on a bone?
Will (noun) have	walked	through the park?
Will we have	gone	on the bus?
Will they have	flown	on the 7th?
Will (nouns) have	looked	through their books?

WITH TRANSITIVE VERBS

This verb form uses the past participle adjectives and the present tense version of the verb 'have' to form the tense together with a modal verb and a noun phrase as the object. The modal verb 'will' has been used as it is the most common modal but other modals can be used instead.

Positive Form	Adjective	Noun Phrase
I will have (I'll have)	bought	the newspaper
You will have (you'll have)	seen	the reports
He will have (he'll have)	eaten	some noodles
She will have (she'll have)	sold	insurance
It will have (it'll have)	noticed	the people
(noun) will have ('ll have)	ridden	the bus
We will have (we'll have)	taken	the same route
They will have (they'll have)	spent	their evenings
(nouns) have ('ll have)	studied	the subject

Negative Form	Adjective	Noun Phrase
I will not (won't) have	done	the crossword
You will not (won't) have	known	the answer
He will not (won't) have	brought	people
She will not (won't) have	loved	her own body
It will not (won't) have	liked	the food
(noun) will not (won't) have	taught	the students
We will not (won't) have	bought	French fries
They will not (won't) have	caught	the bus
(nouns) will not (won't) have	attended	the meetings

Question Form	Adjective	Noun Phrase
Will I have	had	the attention
Will you have	taken	a shower
Will he have	written	his notes
Will she have	played	the cello
Will it have	dug	holes
Will (noun) have	watched	movies
Will we have	attended	the party
Will they have	driven	their car
Will (nouns) have	found	the hidden posts

FUTURE PERFECT WORKSHEET

Positive Form

I will have
You will have
He will have
She will have
It will have
            will have
We will have
They will have
            will have

Negative Form

I will not have have
You will not have
He will not have
She will not have
It will not have
        will not have
We will not have
They will not have
        will not have

Question Form

Will I have
Will you have
Will he have
Will she have
Will it have
Will   have
Will we have
Will they have
Will   have

Verb Tenses

PRESENT PERFECT WITH MODALS

When modal verbs are used in conjunction with the present perfect tense the resulting construct can be used to talk about events that have happened already that are now effecting the present. In most cases they are used to state that the speaker <u>believes</u> that something has happened, or should have happened, but they may be wrong.

Note that in the positive form the verbs 'have' and 'need' have to match the subject (has/have and need/needs) and in the negative form the verbs 'have, 'need' and 'ought' are prefaced with doesn't (does not) instead of being followed by 'not' like the other modals.

In the examples 'she' has been used as the subject but any person can be used instead.

Positive form	Adjective	Prepositional Phrases	
She **has to** have	worked	in a university	
She **must** have	gone	to the library	
She **needs to** have	studied	in the study room	
She **shall** have	cried	in her room	
She **can** have	slept	on the bed	
She **ought to** have	ran	in the park	
She **should** have	skied	in the snow	
She **could** have	walked	on the path	if...
She **may** have	eaten	at your house	
She **might** have	come	past my house	but...
She **would** have	learned	about her subject	but...
Negative Form	Adjective	Prepositional Phrases	
She **doesn't have to** have	driven	across town	
She **must not** have	cycled	across the campus	
She **doesn't need to** have	dozed	in a chair	
She **shall not** have	eaten	at the cafeteria	
She **can not** have	barked	at strangers	
She **doesn't ought to** have	reached	across the table	
She **should not** have	climbed	up the hills	
She **could not** have	looked	at their books	if...
She **may not** have	written	up his notes	
She **might not** have	played	on her computer	
She **would not** have	served	in the shop	but...

WITH INTRANSITIVE VERBS

Use the following definitions in order to complete the sentences.

have/has to - logical conclusion

need to - state requirements

can - strong possibility

should - regret at not doing something

may - 50% possibility

must - only possible conclusion

shall - 1st person definite

ought to - best course of action

could - 3rd conditional

might - vague (<30%) possibility

would - reason something was not done

Positive form

have/has to have

must have

needs to have

shall have

can have

ought to have

should have

could have   if

may have

might have

would have   but

Negative Form

doesn't have to have

must not have

doesn't need to have

shall not have

can not have

doesn't ought to have

should not have

could not have   if

may not have

might not have

would not have   but

WITH TRANSITIVE VERBS

When modal verbs are used in conjunction with the present perfect tense the resulting construct can be used to talk about events that have happened already that are now effecting the present. In most cases they are used to state that the speaker <u>believes</u> that something has happened, or should have happened, but they may be wrong.

Note that in the positive form the verbs 'have' and 'need' have to match the subject (has/have and need/needs) and in the negative form the verbs 'have, 'need' and 'ought' are prefaced with doesn't (does not) instead of being followed by 'not' like the other modals.

In the examples 'she' has been used as the subject but any person can be used instead.

Positive form	Adjective	Noun Phrase	
She **has to** have	bought	the newspaper	
She **must** have	seen	the reports	
She **needs to** have	eaten	some noodles	
She **shall** have	sold	insurance	
She **can** have	noticed	the people	
She **ought to** have	ridden	the bus	
She **should** have	taken	the same route	
She **could** have	spent	the evening	if...
She **may** have	studied	the subject	
She **might** have	had	the attention	
She **would** have	taken	a shower	but...
Negative Form	adjective	Noun phrase	
She **doesn't have to** have	done	the crossword	
She **must not** have	known	the answer	
She **doesn't need to** have	brought	people	
She **shall not** have	loved	her own body	
She **can not** have	liked	the food	
She **doesn't ought to** have	taught	the students	
She **should not** have	bought	french fries	
She **could not** have	caught	the bus	if...
She **may not** have	attended	the meetings	
She **might not** have	played	the cello	
She **would not** have	written	the notes	but...

PRESENT PERFECT AND MODALS

Use the following definitions in order to complete the sentences.

have/has to - logical conclusion

need to - state requirements

can - strong possibility

should - regret at not doing something

may - 50% possibility

must - only possible conclusion

shall - 1st person definite

ought to - best course of action

could - 3rd conditional

might - vague (<30%) possibility

would - reason something was not done

Positive form

have/has to have

must have

needs to have

shall have

can have

ought to have

should have

could have   if

may have

might have

would have   but

Negative Form

doesn't have to have

must not have

doesn't need to have

shall not have

can not have

doesn't ought to have

should not have

could not have   if

may not have

might not have

would not have   but

PERFECT CONTINUOUS TENSE

None of the previous tense formations can adequately describe how long a continuous action or state has actually lasted. Although this tense wouldn't be commonly used it would be extremely useful. If we refer back to the previous sub-section on continuous tenses, we will see that the present participle ('**ing**') form of adjective is used to describe something that was, is or will be in that state over a period of time. So, it seems logical to use this form when we describe the duration of the state of something. However, we need to add another verb to indicate that we need to know how long the state, caused by the action, has been 'experienced'. Logically we'd use **have**.

For example, let's use this sequence of verbs to create a verb phrase:

She **had been sleeping**

Now that tells us that a female has been in a particular state for a while and that state was asleep. But what it doesn't tell us how long she was in this state. For that, we can add a prepositional phrase (to describe the length of time), or an adverb clause (if an action ended the state), to this to turn it into a sentence. That <u>prepositional phrase</u> can be preceded by the prepositions **since**, to state when she first entered that state (She **had been sleeping** <u>since 8pm</u>), **for**, to state the length of time she was in that state (She **had been sleeping** <u>for 8 hours</u>) or the *adverb clause* markers **until** or **when**, which can be used to describe an event, or action, that stopped her being in that state(She **had been sleeping** *until she woke up* or She **had been sleeping** *when the phone rang*).

These sentences are talking about some state that has already finished (past tense), but if we want to talk about something happening now or has very recently finished (present tense) or something that is going to finish sometime in the future (future tense), we can change the verb phrase like so:

She **has been sleeping** <u>for 8 hours</u>. (present - as she is still sleeping)

She **will have been sleeping** <u>for 8 hours</u> *when she is awoken*. (future)

Note the use of an additional adverb clause, **when she is awoken**, to say when the state is likely to finish. We could have used another prepositional phrase like, **at 6 am tomorrow morning**, instead of the adverb clause.

PERFECT CONTINUOUS USES

Present Perfect Continuous

Present Perfect Continuous is used to show that something started in the past and has continued up until now. It is also used to describe something that happened a short time before or has recently finished.

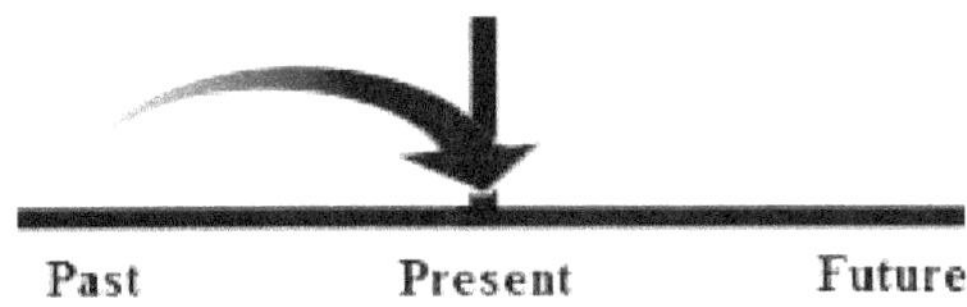

Past Perfect Continuous

Past perfect continuous can be used to discuss the cause (or the effect) of something. It is mainly used to discuss something that happened before but has now finished.

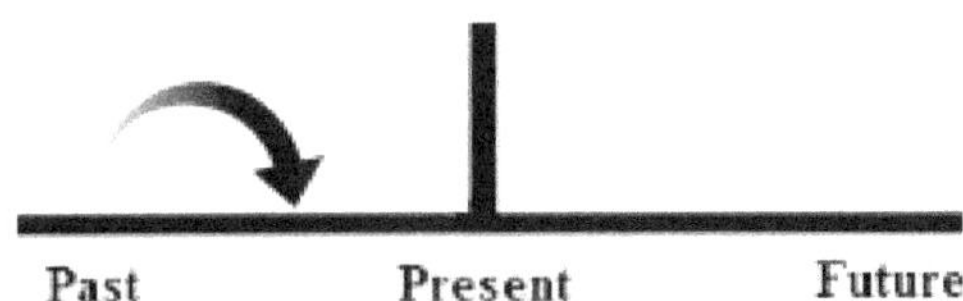

Future Perfect Continuous

Future perfect continuous can be used to give a reason for something happening in the future. It can also be used to describe how long something that will finish in the future is likely to be going on for. The tense can take one of two forms: will have been +ing, usually used to describe duration of a spontaneous action and be going to have been +ing, used to describe the duration of a thought out action.

PRESENT PERFECT CONTINUOUS

Creation: Used to describe continuing actions in the present with an emphasis on the duration rather than when it is happening.

be (verb)	not (optional)	been	present participle

Examples: I have been waiting for two hours *or* Bill has not been playing this morning.

Note the main differences between the present perfect and present perfect continuous is that the present perfect uses a single auxiliary verb (have) and the past participle of the verb, whereas present perfect continuous uses two auxiliary verbs (have and been) and the present participle.

Use this tense to describe the following:

Duration from the past until now: use it to show that something started in the past and has continued up until now. Any time duration from the past can be used right up until this very instant.

Example: The lecture **has been going on** for hours (**go on** is a phrasal verb that is commonly used to indicate that the action was taking too long).

Recently or just lately: Used without the duration (which is optional in this tense), the tense has a more general meaning of "lately." You can use the adverbs *lately* or *recently* to emphasize this meaning.

Examples: What **have** you **been doing** lately *or* Have you **been practicing** your English recently?

A continuous action taking place from a fixed point in time: used with either **for** or **since** (for may be used with any tense whereas since is used only with perfect tenses) to describe a continuous action that has been going on since a fixed point in time (since) or over a certain duration (for). Note the time can be in the absolute (since 7 p.m.) or abstract (for ages).

Examples:

I **have been writing** since 9 p.m. last night. (From a fixed point in time)

He **has not been working** since he lost his job (and he isn't working now)

They **have been studying** all day (and they are still studying)

Tiffany **has been waiting** for ages (and she's still waiting)

Defining a cause: This tense can be used as part of complex sentences containing adverbial clauses to describe why something happened using a coordinating conjunction such as because.

Example: I am sitting down because **I have been working** hard all morning.

WITH INTRANSITIVE VERBS

This verb form uses the present participle adjectives, the present tense version of the verb 'have' and the past participle of 'be' to form the tense. The prepositional phrases, shown below, say what was being done and duration prepositional phrases (prefaced with for or since) or adverb clauses (prefaced with clause markers like until or when) should also be added (but are not shown in the table).

Positive Form	Adjective	Prepositional Phrase
I have (I've) been	working	on my project
You have (you've) been	going	to my house
He has (he's) been	studying	in his room
She has (she's) been	crying	at the sad movie
It has (it's) been	sleeping	in its kennel
(noun) has ('s) been	running	around the track
We have (we've) been	skiing	through the snow
They have (they've) been	walked	to their classroom
(nouns) have ('ve) been	reading	for their thesis

Negative Form	Adjective	Prepositional Phrase
I have not (haven't) been	driving	to the party
You have not (haven't) been	cycling	across the campus
He has not (hasn't) been	dozing	in a chair
She has not (hasn't) been	eating	in the restaurant
It has not (hasn't) been	barking	at the stranger
(noun) has not (hasn't) been	reaching	for the salt
We have not (haven't) been	climbing	up the hill
They have not (haven't) been	looking	at the rainbow
(nouns) have not (haven't) been	serving	at the shop

Question Form	Adjective	Prepositional Phrase
Have I been	eating	at your house?
Have you been	coming	to my party?
Has he been	writing	down the details?
Has she been	reading	through her notes?
Has it been	chewing	on a bone?
Has (noun) been	walking	through the park?
Have we been	going	on the bus?
Have they been	flying	on the aircraft?
Have (nouns) been	looking	through their books?

WITH TRANSITIVE VERBS

This verb form uses the present participle adjectives, the present tense version of the verb 'have' and the past participle of 'be' to form the tense. Noun phrases are used to form sentences as the object. Duration prepositional phrases (prefaced with for or since) or adverb clauses (prefaced with clause markers like until or when) should also be added. The shaded abstract verbs shouldn't be used in this tense, use the perfect tense instead.

Positive Form	Adjective	Noun Phrase
I have (I've) been	buying	the newspaper
You have (you've) been	seeing	the reports
He has (he's) been	eating	some noodles
She has (she's) been	selling	insurance
It has (it's) been	noticing	the people
(noun) has ('s) been	riding	the bus
We have (we've) been	taking	the same route
They have (they've) been	spending	their evenings
(nouns) have ('ve) been	studying	the subject
Negative Form	Adjective	Noun Phrase
I have not (haven't) been	doing	the crossword
You have not (haven't) been	knowing	the answer
He has not (hasn't) been	bringing	people
She has not (hasn't) been	loving	her own body
It has not (hasn't) been	liking	the food
(noun) has not (hasn't) been	teaching	the students
We have not (haven't) been	buying	French fries
They have not (haven't) been	catching	the bus
(nouns) have not (haven't) been	attending	the meetings
Question Form	Adjective	Noun Phrase
Have I been	having	the attention
Have you been	taking	a shower
Has he been	writing	his notes
Has she been	playing	the cello
Has it been	digging	holes
Has (noun) been	watching	movies
Have we been	attending	the party
Have they been	driving	their car
Have (nouns) been	finding	the hidden posts

PRESENT PERFECT CONTINUOUS

Positive Form

I have been

You have been

He has been

She has been

It has been

has been

We have been

They have been

have been

Negative Form

I have not been

You have not been

He has not been

She has not been

It has not been

has not been

We have not been

They have not been

have not been

Question Form

Have I been

Have you been

Has he been

Has she been

Has it been

Has been

Have we been

Have they been

Have been

PAST PERFECT CONTINUOUS

Creation: This tense is used to describe continuing actions in the past that took place before another action in the past. It takes the form:

had (verb)	not (optional)	been (aux)	present participle

Examples: I **had been sitting** here for two hours before you arrived or **She had not been** skiing before.

Note that this tense differs from past perfect in that the action is usually over a longer time period. The **'had not'** (in negative sentences) is usually contracted to **hadn't**. So the second example sentence would normally be **She hadn't been skiing** before. The past conjugation **had** is used irrespective of whether it is first, second or third person.

Use this tense to describe:

Duration of something before something in the past: use this tense to describe the **duration** of an action in the past that was interrupted or finished by a subsequent action.

Examples: How long **had** you **been waiting** before the train came in? *or* Michelle **had been worrying** for 3 months before she got her exam results.

Cause of something in the past: this tense can be used to show both the cause and the effect of something.

Example: I missed the plane as **I had been sitting** in traffic for two hours

Effect of something in the past: this tense can also be used to state the effect of something based on a previous incident.

Example: I had been lying in a hospital bed after I fell off my motorcycle.

Past Perfect Continuous versus Present Perfect Continuous

At first glance the two tenses are almost identical in both construction and meaning. The difference being that in past perfect continuous the action has already taken place and has already finished in the past; whereas with present perfect continuous the action is either still happening or has only just finished. Consider the following sentences:

I **was** tired as **I had been working** all day. (Past Perfect Continuous)
I **am** tired as **I have been working** all day. (Present Perfect Continuous)

The first sentence gave a reason for an event sometime in the past that has now finished; the second gives a reason for a current event.

WITH INTRANSITIVE VERBS

This verb form uses the present participle adjectives and the past tense version of the verb 'have' and the past participle of 'be' to form the tense. You can use this verb form, plus if, to create conditional statements (If I had not been eating at the time, I would not have ignored the telephone). The question form is usually used to talk about third conditionals and not for framing questions.

Positive Form	Adjective	Prepositional Phrase
I had (I'd) been	working	on my project
You had (you'd) been	going	to my house
He had (he'd) been	studying	in his room
She had (she'd) been	crying	at the sad movie
It had (it'd) been	sleeping	in its kennel
(noun) had ('d) been	running	around the track
We had (we'd been	skiing	through the snow
They had (they'd) been	walked	to their classroom
(nouns) had ('d) been	reading	for their thesis

Negative Form	Adjective	Prepositional Phrase
I had not (hadn't) been	driving	to the party
You had not (hadn't) been	cycling	across the campus
He had not (hadn't) been	dozing	in a chair
She had not (hadn't) been	eating	in the restaurant
It had not (hadn't) been	barking	at the stranger
(noun) had not (hadn't) been	reaching	for the salt
We had not (hadn't) been	climbing	up the hill
They had not (hadn't) been	looking	at the rainbow
(nouns) had not (hadn't) been	serving	at the shop

Question Form	Adjective	Prepositional Phrase
Had I been	eating	at your house?
Had you been	coming	to my party?
Had he been	writing	down the details?
Had she been	reading	through her notes?
Had it been	chewing	on a bone?
Had (noun) been	walking	through the park?
Had we been	going	on the bus?
Had they been	flying	on the aircraft?
Had (nouns) been	looking	through their books?

WITH TRANSITIVE VERBS

This verb form uses the present participle adjectives and the past tense version of the verb 'have' and the present participle of 'be' to form the tense. You can use this verb form, plus if, to create conditional statements (If she had been attending her classes then she would have known about the exam). The question form is usually used to talk about third conditionals and not for framing questions.

Positive Form	Adjective	Noun Phrase
I had (I'd) been	buying	the newspaper
You had (you'd) been	seeing	the reports
He had (he'd) been	eating	some noodles
She had (she'd) been	selling	insurance
It had (it'd) been	noticing	the people
(noun) had ('d) been	riding	the bus
We had (we'd) been	taking	the same route
They had (they'd) been	spending	their evenings
(nouns) had ('d) been	studying	the subject
Negative Form	**Adjective**	**Noun Phrase**
I had not (hadn't) been	doing	the crossword
You had not (hadn't) been	knowing	the answer
He had not (hadn't) been	bringing	people
She had not (hadn't) been	loving	her own body
It had not (hadn't) been	liking	the food
(noun) had not (hadn't) been	teaching	the students
We had not (hadn't) been	buying	French fries
They had not (hadn't) been	catching	the bus
(nouns) had not (hadn't) been	attending	the meetings
Question Form	**Adjective**	**Noun Phrase**
Had I been	having	the attention...
Had you been	taking	a shower...
Had he been	writing	his notes...
Had she been	playing	the cello...
Had it been	digging	holes...
Had (noun) been	watching	movies...
Had we been	attending	the party...
Had they been	driving	their car...
Had (nouns) been	finding	the hidden posts...

PAST PERFECT CONTINUOUS

I had been
You had been
He had been
She had been
It had been
     had been
We had been
They had been
     had been

I had not been
You had not been
He had not been
She had not been
It had not been
     had not been
We had not been
They had not been
     had not been

Had I been
Had you been
Had he been
Had she been
Had it been
Had   been
Had we been
Had they been
Had   been

FUTURE PERFECT CONTINUOUS

Creation: This tense is used to describe continuing actions in the future that will take place before another action in the future.

will (modal)	not (optional)	have (aux)	been (aux)	present participle

Examples: She **will not have been working** today *or* I **will have been singing** for ten hours by tonight.

Note **She will not** can be contracted to become **she won't** (informal) or **she'll not** (semi-formal) and **I will** can be contracted to **I'll**. As with other future tenses alternative modals can be used to change the intent.

Use this tense to describe:

Duration of an action before another action in the future: Use to describe something that will happen up to or until another event or action in the future. It is like both present perfect continuous and the past perfect continuous but, unlike them, it stops at a prescribed point in the future.

Examples: At this rate **I'll have been waiting** for two hours by the time she arrives *or* He'**ll have been working** here for 30 years by the time he retires.

Cause or effect of something in the future: can also be used (together with the word **because**) to show cause or effect of an event or action at a predetermined point in the future.

Examples: She **will have been waiting** for ages because I forgot to pick her up *or* He **will have been walking** for hours because his car broke down.

Future Continuous versus Future Perfect Continuous

While the two tenses may look similar they have different meanings. Future continuous emphasizes a point in time, whereas future perfect continuous emphasizes the duration of an action. For **Example:**

First the future continuous:

I **will be sleeping** at 8 p.m. (At that point in time I will be asleep)

Now the future perfect continuous:

I **will have been sleeping** since 6. (The duration is from 6 until now)

Two further examples show how the duration is highlighted in future perfect continuous:

I **will be waiting** when you arrive. (future continuous)

I **will have been waiting** <u>for two hours</u> when you arrive.(future perfect continuous - Note the <u>time period</u>).

WITH INTRANSITIVE VERBS

This tense uses a prepositional phrase, to describe how long it will happen for (phrase 1) or to describe the action, and another one, or an adverb or adverb clause, to say when it will finish (phrase 2). Note, abbreviations of will ('ll) have been used to save space - abbreviations are not used in questions. Alternative modal verbs can be used to change the liability, possibility, permission or obligation.

Positive Form	Adjective	Phrase 1	Phrase 2
I'll have been	eating	for 2 hours	at 9 p.m.
You'll have been	applying	for months	by the new year.
He'll have been	sleeping	for 8 hours	by tonight.
She'll have been	asking	every day	for weeks.
It'll have been	missing	for 12 hours	by nightfall.
(noun)'ll have been	cooking	since noon	today.
We'll have been	emailing	all day	since 8 am.
They'll have been	searching	for 3 days	by Friday.
(nouns)'ll have been	studying	for 8 hours	at midnight.

Negative Form	Adjective	Phrase 1	Phrase 2
I won't have been	surfing	for a week	by tomorrow.
You won't have been	fishing	for a month	by next Friday.
He won't have been	starting	for 2 hours	in a minute.
She won't have been	waiting	for weeks	by the end.
It won't have been	scratching	for hours	by tonight.
(noun) won't have been	running	for ten days	by this evening.
We won't have been	entering	for five years	by next year.
They won't have been	questioning	for 2 weeks	by tomorrow.
(nouns) won't have been	delivering	for 3 weeks	by today.

Question Form	Adjective	Phrase 1	Phrase 2
Will I have been	talking	for 2 hours	by 8 p.m.?
Will you have been	washing	for 3 hours	when I arrive?
Will he have been	designing	for days	by the end?
Will she have been	browsing	for hours	in the morning?
Will it have been	chewing	on its bone	until it is gone?
Will (noun) have been	boring	for hours	by the finish?
Will we have been	running	for ages	by tomorrow?
Will they have been	writing	for hours	by this evening?
Will (nouns) have been	driving	for ten hours	by tonight?

WITH TRANSITIVE VERBS

This tense uses a noun phrase to describe the object of the sentence (phrase 1) and another one, or an adverb or adverb clause, to say when it will finish or how long it is likely to last (phrase 2). These would be followed by a further phrase (not shown below) to show the end point. Note, abbreviations of will ('ll) have been used to save space, they are not used in questions. The abstract verbs can be used in this tense.

Positive Form	Adjective	Phrase 1	Phrase 2
I'll have been	buying	the paper	for 2 years
You'll have been	seeing	the reports	for months
He'll have been	eating	some noodles	for 8 hours
She'll have been	selling	insurance	every day
It'll have been	noticing	the people	for 12 hours
(noun)'ll have been	riding	the bus	since noon
We'll have been	taking	the train	all day
They'll have been	spending	their money	for 3 days
(nouns)'ll have been	studying	the subject	for 8 hours
Negative Form	Adjective	Phrase 1	Phrase 2
I won't have been	doing	my work	for a week
You won't have been	knowing	the answer	for a month
He won't have been	bringing	people	for 2 hours
She won't have been	loving	her own body	for weeks
It won't have been	liking	the food	for hours
(noun) won't have been	teaching	the students	for ten days
We won't have been	buying	French fries	for five years
They won't have been	catching	the bus	for 2 weeks
(nouns) won't have been	attending	the meetings	for 3 weeks
Question Form	Adjective	Phrase 1	Phrase 2
Will I have been	having	the attention	for 2 hours
Will you have been	taking	a shower	for 3 hours
Will he have been	writing	his notes	for days
Will she have been	playing	the cello	for hours
Will it have been	digging	hole	on its bone
Will (noun) have been	watching	movie	for hours
Will we have been	attending	the party	for ages
Will they have been	driving	their car	for hours
Will (nouns) have been	finding	the web posts	for ten hours

FUTURE PERFECT CONTINUOUS

Positive Form

I had been
You had been
He had been
She had been
It had been
        had been
We had been
They had been
        had been

Negative Form

I had not been
You had not been
He had not been
She had not been
It had not been
        had not been
We had not been
They had not been
        had not been

Question Form

Had I been
Had you been
Had he been
Had she been
Had it been
Had   been
Had we been
Had they been
Had   been

ACTIVE VERSUS PASSIVE VOICE

The voice (also known as the diathesis) of a verb describes the relationship between the action (or state) that the verb describes and the participants that are affected by it; for example the subject(s) and object(s). When the subject is the thing that does the action, or describes their state, the verb is regarded as active voice.

When the subject is the target of the action, in other words things are done **to them** rather that **by them**, the verb is regarded as passive voice. Put another way, active is used to describe what action the subject is doing, whereas passive is used to show that the subject is supine and has little or no control over the action or what is being done to them. Note, that if the person performing the action is required then a prepositional phrase is used (often using **by**). For **Example:**

He **was boring** everybody	Active as the subject is imposing boredom on others
I **was bored** <u>by</u> his speech	Passive as the subject has boredom imposed on them

One very common use of the passive voice is to show the direction of something in an exchange. The following examples, use the verb **'give'**:

I **was giving** some money <u>to</u> her.	(Active voice)
I **was given** some money <u>by</u> her.	(Passive voice)

In the first example, the **present continuous** tense was used to show that it was me that was supplying the money, whereas, in the second example, in the **simple past** tense, it was her who was supplying the money to me. Note the use of the **prepositions**, which confirm the direction the money is moving in.

Passive voice verb structures are generally longer (having an extra auxiliary verb) than their active voice equivalents. For this reason they are becoming less popular in printed publications, such as professional journals, where space may be limited. Some (American) academics are arguing that we stop using passive voice (and perfect tense) to make English simpler but that risks losing the richness of the language.

ACTIVE VERSUS PASSIVE VOICE

Comparing active and passive voices

The table below shows how the two voices are constructed using all of the tenses. In the active voice the speaker is generally taking responsibility for undertaking the action; whereas, in the passive voice the action is generally being undertaken by unnamed individuals and it is implied that no-one is actually taking overall responsibility for undertaking the action. In these business conversations the active tenses are generally used by smaller businesses to give a personal touch and passive voice is used by larger companies and the public sector in order to avoid personalisation.

Tense	Active Voice	Passive Voice
Simple Present	I **send** packages all over the world.	Packages **are sent** all over the world.
Present Continuous	I **am sending** it to you today	It **is being sent** to you today.
Present Perfect	I **have made** the arrangements to send it.	The arrangements **have been made** to send it.
Present Perfect Continuous	I **have been making** the arrangements to send it for a week.	The arrangements **have been being made** to send it for a week.

Simple Past	I **sent** it to you yesterday	It **was sent** yesterday.
Past Continuous	I **was working** on your order	Your order **was being worked** on.
Past Perfect	I **had sent** it already.	It **had been sent** already.
Past Perfect Continuous	I **had been sending** it but then I had a problem.	It **had been being sent** when there was a problem.

Simple Future	I **will send** it to you tomorrow.	It **will be sent** tomorrow.
Future Continuous	I **will be sending** it via a courier.	It **will be being sent** via a courier.
Future Perfect	You **will have received** it by next week.	It **will have been received** by you next week.
Future Perfect Continuous	I **will have been sending it every day** for a month by next week.	It **will have been being sent** every day for a month by next week.

MAKING VERBS PASSIVE

The following covers the 'rules' of making verbs passive. Most verbs can be used in the passive voice, but not all verbs.

Auxiliary verbs are not used as the main verb in the passive voice. So, you can't say something like, the house ~~has been been~~ like this for a long time.

Another group of verbs that generally cannot be made passive are most **state verbs**, even if they can be used as transitive verbs. So, you can't say things like, the bag ~~was belonged~~ by the boy. However, there are some state verbs that are commonly passive. For example, the verbs **know** (This fact **is known** by most people) and **misunderstand** (What the professor said **was misunderstood** by the students). In addition, there are verbs that are almost always passive, such as **born** (He **was born** into a wealthy family), **populate** (The island **was populated** by snakes), **ship** (The product **was shipped** yesterday) and **strew** (Papers **were strewn** all over the floor).

Some active verbs often have a passive meaning. For example, the verb **read** can have a passive meaning as in, The sign **read** "do not smoke", as can the verb **show** as in: The map **doesn't show** how to get there. In addition, if the verbs **need, require** or **want** are followed by a gerund they assume a passive meaning. For example; The car **needs fixing** (by somebody), the table **requires polishing** *or* the dog **wants walking**.

Finally, some verbs are used, in an idiomatic form, in the passive voice but actually have an active meaning. For example, Are you finished? Which, strictly speaking should be, have you finished? Note, in this form the sentence is used to ask, usually sarcastically, whether someone has stopped ranting, nagging or talking nonsense.

Generally, if the verb is transitive verb, it can be made passive. However, if the verb is intransitive, then, as a rule, it cannot be made passive. So, for example the following verbs should not be made passive: **arise, arrive, consist, depend, exist, fall, happen, occur, result, rise, run** and **sleep**; <u>unless</u> they are used in phrasal verbs. The table on the opposite page demonstrates how this works.

PASSIVE INTRANSITIVE VERBS

The following are common intransitive verbs and together with an adverb (Adv.) they are converted to phrasal verbs so they can be used in the passive voice; albeit with a changed meaning in most cases.

Verb	Adv.	Examples in the passive voice
agree	to	The treaty **was agreed to** by all parties.
appear	to	The people **were appeared to** by a ghost.
arrive	at	The venue **was arrived at** by the guests.
become	of	What **was become of** him is a mystery.
belong	to	The club **was belonged to** by many people.
consist	in	The city's fame **is consisted in** its art.
cough	up	The money **was coughed up** eventually.
cry	out	The news **was cried out** by the town crier.
die	from	Black death **was died from** in the 1600s.
disappear	into	The gloomy forest **was disappeared into.**
emerge	onto	The stage **was emerged onto** by the actor.
exist	on	Rice **is existed on** by many Asian people.
fall	out of	The aircraft **was fallen out of** by the victim.
happen	upon	The crime **was happened upon** by a witness.
inquire	into	The crime **was inquired into** by the police.
laugh	at	The teacher **was laughed at** by his class.
live	in	The house **was lived in** by my family.
look	on	Her ideas **were looked on** favourably by us.
respond	to	The memo **will be responded to** later.
run	up	The debt **was run up** by the bankrupt firm.
sit	on	This chair **was sat on** after it was cleaned.
sleep	in	This bed **was slept in** by a famous person.
smile	at	I **was smiled at** by a pretty girl.
stand	by	He **was stood by** during his trial by her.
stay	in	The hotel **was stayed in** by my family.
wait	on	The customers **were waited on** by her.

In the tense example pages the adverbs were chosen so the phrasal verb meaning stayed close to the original meaning wherever possible.

WHEN TO USE PASSIVE VOICE

Where the person or thing performing the action is unknown:

Used for: Statements from the Police about results of a crime where the perpetrator hasn't been caught yet and in newspapers where an action has been undertaken and no-one is sure about who (or what) did it.

Examples: The store **was robbed** yesterday *or* The bridge **will be demolished** tomorrow.

Where something is of relevance to everyone:

Used for: Describing actions that are relevant to everybody.

Examples: Laws **are meant** to be observed *or* A graduate level education **is required.**

When writing in a scientific genre:

Used for: Texts such as lab reports and scientific research papers.

Example: This research **has been undertaken** to find a cure for HIV/AIDS.

Where the identity of the person or thing doing the action is not relevant or is not required:

Used for: Reporting things like the results of research (such as clinical trials).

Example: Sildenafil citrate, Viagra, **was found** to help cure erectile dysfunction.

Where the thing being referred to is obliquely named:

Used for: Not naming the thing that is under discussion, where the name is not known, is hinted at or compared with.

Examples: The software **being used** kept crashing and losing all of the work. (Unknown software).

It **is not certain** what the software was called but it was sold by Serif. (Hinted at)

It **was agreed** that it wasn't as bad as Word though. (Unknown compared with known product).

WHEN TO USE PASSIVE VOICE

Where the person or thing undertaking the action must be kept vague:

Used for: Avoiding naming the person who made a mistake so it avoids embarrassment or censure. Government officials often use this voice to cover up failures or to promise vaguely defined further action to avoid a repetition of the failure.

Examples: The flash drive, containing everyone's tax details, **was left** on the train.

Lessons **will be learned** (describing an action that can't be quantified or checked and, as such, is very commonly used in government departments).

The procedures **will be studied** to avoid this problem in future (or maybe they won't! Who will ever know?)

Where the effect of something new is being reported on:

Used for: Things like announcing the findings and/or consequences of any new procedure.

Examples: The new traffic system **has been found** to decrease the number of traffic jams.

Cannabis **has been proven** to reduce the possibility of contracting cancer.

Where someone is taking responsibility for an action and wants to be forgiven:

Used for: Admitting responsibility when asked who did something.

Examples: I'm sorry, the window **was broken** by me.

I apologize, the remark **was ill considered.**

When something is directed at somebody:

Used for: Showing who something was directed at.

Examples: The problem **was brought** to my attention.

The insults **were thrown** at the politician who embezzled the money.

PRESENT SIMPLE PASSIVE

Creation: In most cases this tense is used to describe current actions by third parties that affect the subject. It takes the form:

be (aux)	**not** (if negative)	**past participle**

The person doing the action does not need to be named, but if they must be included in the sentence then add **by** + subject

Example: The lecture **is given** *by* the Professor or It **is eaten** *by* the dog.

Use this tense to describe the following:

Repeated Actions undertaken by unknown people: Use the simple present to express the idea that an action is repeated or mundane. The action can be anything such as a habit, daily event or a scheduled event. It can also be something that someone often forgets to do.

Examples: Cultural events **are scheduled** for every day this week *or* Wedding anniversaries **are forgotten** by most men

Causes: It can be used to indicate that speaker believes what they are saying is true, whether it is or not, and often giving the reason (using *by*).

Examples: Food poisoning **is** <u>mainly</u> **caused** *by* bad kitchen hygiene.

Imminent events created by others: Can be used to announce the imminent arrival, departure or occurrence of something.

Examples: The storm **is expected** soon *or* The exam **is scheduled** for today.

Something happening now to somebody or something: Can be used to announce an immediate event. Note that present continuous is a better tense to use for describing immediate events as it creates more urgency. For **Example:**

Dogs **are abandoned** at the pound.   (Present simple)
Dogs **are being abandoned** at the pound. (Present continuous)

Something that is not only happening now: Unlike repeated or habitual actions it will refer to events that <u>could</u> happen both now and in the future.

Example: Team meetings **are planned** to take place every Friday.

To indicate that the subjects gets, or is compelled to do, something: In the first example it's <u>a thing</u> the subject gets; whereas, in the second it's <u>an action</u> (indicated by the <u>infinitive</u>) that the subject is compelled to do.

Examples: I **am given** <u>a car</u> by my company as I need it for my job.
          He **is made** <u>to wash</u> his hands before he has dinner.

WITH INTRANSITIVE VERBS

Intransitive verbs are not used to create passive voice on their own but can be used in phrasal verbs. The optional column below describes the person or people that are undertaking the action. The prepositional phrase in the question form describes where or when the action takes place. Note, the subject (first column) is a noun phrase.

Positive Form	(Phrasal) Verb	Optional
The university	is worked in	by me
The library	is gone to	by you
The study room	is studied in	by him
Her room	is cried in	by her
Its kennel	is slept in	by it
The park	is run in	by (noun)
The snow	is skied in	by us
The path	is walked on	by them
Their subject	is learned about	by (nouns)

Negative Form	(Phrasal) Verb	Optional
The party	is not driven to	by me
The campus	is not cycled across	by you
The heater	is not dozed next to	by him
Her school	is not eaten at	by her
His home	is not barked near	by it
The salt	is not reached for	by (noun)
The national park	is not climbed in	by us
Their books	are not looked at	by them
The shop	is not served in	by (nouns)

Question Form	(Phrasal) Verb	Prepositional Phrase
Is your house	eaten at	in the evening?
Is my house	come past	in the morning?
Are the stairs	walked up	after his class?
Is her computer	played on	at night?
Is a bone	chewed on	in its kennel?
Is a bridge	walked under	on his way home?
Is the party	gone to	in the evening?
Is the aircraft	flown away on	on the 17th?
Are their iPads	looked at	under their desks?

WITH TRANSITIVE VERBS

This verb structure uses a present tense version of be, that matches the subject, together with the past participle of the descriptive verb. The 'person' refers to who is the beneficiary/actor of the action. In the question form the preposition may need to be converted into an adjective for inclusion in the subject noun phrase in order to make sense (see the first person question form using 'had').

Noun Phrase	Verb	Preposition	Person
The newspaper	is bought	at the local shop	by me.
The reports	is seen	from your boss	by you.
Some noodles	are eaten	at lunchtime	by him.
Life insurance	is sold	from her office	by her.
The people	is noticed	in the park	by it.
The bus	is ridden	to the office	by (noun).
The same route	is taken	in the morning	by us.
Their evenings	are spent	in the coffee shop	by them.
The subjects	are studied	in their books	by (nouns)
Noun phrase	Verb	Preposition	Person
The crossword	is not done	in the morning	by me.
The answer	is not known	to my question	by you.
People	is not brought	to the meeting	by him.
Her own body	is not loved	at the moment	by her.
The food	is not liked	in its bowl	by it.
The students	is not taught	on Friday	by (noun).
French fries	are not bought	at any time	by us.
The bus	is not caught	in the morning	by them.
The meetings	are not attended	in the office	by (nouns).
Question	Verb	Preposition	Person
Is the class's attention	had	(See noun phrase)	by me?
Is a shower	taken	in the mornings	by you?
Are his notes	written	during his class	by him?
Is the cello	played	in the orchestra	by her?
Are holes	dug	in the garden	by it?
Are movies	watched	after work	by (noun)?
Is the party	attended	at the club	by us?
Is their car	driven	on the footpath	by them?
Are the hidden posts	found	on the website	by (nouns)?

SIMPLE PRESENT PASSIVE

Positive Form		
		by me.
		by you.
		by him.
		by her.
		by it.
		by .
		by us.
		by them.
		by

Negative Form		
	not	by me.
	not	by you.
	not	by him.
	not	by her.
	not	by it.
	not	by .
	not	by us.
	not	by them.
	not	by

Question Form		
(Am/Is/Are)		by me?
(Am/Is/Are)		by you?
(Am/Is/Are)		by him?
(Am/Is/Are)		by her?
(Am/Is/Are)		by it?
(Am/Is/Are)		by ?
(Am/Is/Are)		by us?
(Am/Is/Are)		by them?
(Am/Is/Are)		by ?

PAST SIMPLE PASSIVE

Creation: In most cases this tense is used to describe actions undertaken by others in the past.

be	not (if negative)	past participle

He **was misled** by her *or* The project **was not completed** on time
Use this tense to describe the following:
To show someone received something: use this tense to say that someone was given or awarded something.
Examples: He **was awarded** a medal for bravery *or* I **was given** a new tie
Action completed in the past by others: use this tense to express the idea that an action started and finished at a specific time in the past and is now over. The time may or may not be specified.
Examples: The house **was abandoned** by the owners *(unknown time)*
          Yesterday, my dinner **was cooked** for me *(known time)*
A sequence of completed actions by unknown people: This tense can be used to list completed actions in the past. Note, the person doing the actions is not mentioned.
Example: The tour bus **was brought** to the hotel, then it **was driven** to the beach and later it **was returned** to the depot.
Longer action in the past undertaken by other people: use with a longer action, usually indicated by a timescale, which was started and stopped in the past.
Examples: The car **was used** by them for two years.
          The gun **was fired** every day for a month.
Repetitive actions that were undertaken by previous generations: used to describe a habit or hobby which stopped in the past. It can have the same meaning as "used to."
Example: 'Thou' **was used** instead of you before it went out of fashion.
Past facts: used to describe past facts which are no longer true.
Examples: The abacus **was used** to do calculations before calculators became common. When America **was** first **discovered**; only Native Americans lived there.
Where time or place are mentioned in other people's actions: If the time when an event happened, and/or the place where it took place, are mentioned (usually using prepositional phrases) then use the past simple tense. **Examples:**
The first superman comic **was published** in 1939.   *(time)*
The first automat **was opened** in 1902 in Philadelphia. *(time and place)*

WITH INTRANSITIVE VERBS

Intransitive verbs are not used to create passive voice on their own but can be used in phrasal verbs. This structure uses the past form of be and the past participle of the descriptive verb. The optional column below describes the person or people that are undertaking the action. Note, the subject (first column) is a noun phrase.

Positive Form	(Phrasal) Verb	Optional
The university	was worked in	by me
The library	was gone to	by you
The study room	was studied in	by him
Her room	was cried in	by her
Its kennel	was slept in	by it
The park	was run in	by (noun)
The snow	was skied in	by us
The path	was walked on	by them
Their subject	was learned about	by (nouns)
Negative Form	**(Phrasal) Verb**	**Optional**
The party	was not driven to	by me
The campus	was not cycled across	by you
The heater	was not dozed next to	by him
Her school	was not eaten at	by her
His home	was not barked near	by it
The salt	was not reached for	by (noun)
The national park	was not climbed in	by us
Their books	were not looked at	by them
The shop	was not served in	by (nouns)
Question Form	**(Phrasal) Verb**	**Optional**
Was your house	eaten at	by me?
Was my house	come past	by you?
Were the stairs	walked up	by him?
Was her computer	played on	by her?
Was a bone	chewed on	by it?
Was a bridge	walked under	by (noun)?
Was the party	gone to	by us?
Was the aircraft	flown away on	by them?
Were their iPads	looked at	by (nouns)?

WITH TRANSITIVE VERBS

This verb structure uses a past tense version of **be**, that matches the subject, together with the past participle of the descriptive verb. The 'person' refers to who is the beneficiary/actor of the action. In the question form the preposition may need to be converted into an adjective for inclusion in the subject noun phrase in order to make sense (see the first person question form using 'had').

Noun Phrase	Verb	Preposition	Person
The newspaper	was bought	at the local shop.	by me.
The reports	was seen	from your boss.	by you.
Some noodles	were eaten	at lunchtime.	by him.
Life insurance	was sold	from her office.	by her.
The people	was noticed	in the park.	by it.
The bus	was ridden	to the office.	by (noun).
The same route	was taken	in the morning.	by us.
Their evenings	were spent	in the coffee shop.	by them.
The subjects	were studied	in their books.	by (nouns)
Noun phrase	**Verb**	**Preposition**	**Person**
The crossword	was not done	in the morning.	by me.
The answer	was not known	to my question.	by you.
People	was not brought	to the meeting.	by him.
Her own body	was not loved	at the moment.	by her.
The food	was not liked	in its bowl.	by it.
The students	was not taught	on Friday.	by (noun).
French fries	were not bought	at any time.	by us.
The bus	was not caught	in the morning.	by them.
The meetings	were not attended	in the office.	by (nouns).
Question	**Verb**	**Preposition**	**Person**
Was the class's attention	had	(See noun phrase)	by me?
Was a shower	taken	in the mornings?	by you?
Were his notes	written	during his class?	by him?
Was the cello	played	in the orchestra?	by her?
Were holes	dug	in the garden?	by it?
Were movies	watched	after work?	by (noun)?
Was the party	attended	at the club?	by us?
Was their car	driven	on the footpath?	by them?
Were the hidden posts	found	on the website?	by (nouns)?

SIMPLE PAST PASSIVE

Positive Form		
		by me.
		by you.
		by him.
		by her.
		by it.
		by .
		by us.
		by them.
		by

Negative Form		
	not	by me.
	not	by you.
	not	by him.
	not	by her.
	not	by it.
	not	by .
	not	by us.
	not	by them.
	not	by

Question Form		
(Was/Were)		by me?
(Was/Were)		by you?
(Was/Were)		by him?
(Was/Were)		by her?
(Was/Were)		by it?
(Was/Were)		by ?
(Was/Were)		by us?
(Was/Were)		by them?
(Was/Were)		by ?

FUTURE SIMPLE PASSIVE

Creation: This tense is used to describe future actions or predictions that are beyond the control of the subject. It takes the form:

will (modal)	**not** (if negative)	**be** (aux)	**past participle**

Examples: I **will be picked** up later *or* She **will not be swayed** by nasty comments or gossip

Note that the 1st auxiliary verb is a modal verb and so other modal verbs, other than **will,** can be used to provide strength, politeness or special meaning to the sentence.

Use this tense to describe

Expressing a voluntary action by somebody: use this tense (with the word **will**) to describe an action that will be undertaken in the future. It can also be used to try to obtain a promise of a commitment. For **Example:**

The mission **will be undertaken** by NASA (future action)
He **will be asked** to give a presentation (obtain a commitment promise)

Immediate action by somebody: use this tense to supply details of an action that will be started straight away. Note that the first example sentence is formal (business) and the second is informal.

Examples: Interviews **will be held** today *or* You**'ll be seen** shortly

Pre-planned events with outcomes decided by others: this tense may be used to talk about opinions about the effects of future actions that may have already been decided at the time of speaking. In this case, the sentence will start with the verbs think *or* believe. **Examples:**

I think he**'ll be beaten** in the finals (the finals will happen)
I believe she**'ll be promoted** this year (promotions will happen)

Expressing a desire not to do something despite pressure from others: use when wanting to say that an unplanned action will not be taking place.

Example: I **will not be bullied** into submission

Giving details of a planned course of action: this tense can be used to outline the details of a plan.

Examples: You **will be informed** about our response later.
He **won't be replaced** when he leaves.

Make a prediction about the future that is beyond anyone's control: use to make a firm prediction about a future course of events.

Example: The earth **will be consumed** in a fireball when the sun explodes.

WITH INTRANSITIVE VERBS

Intransitive verbs are not used to create passive voice on their own but can be used in phrasal verbs. This structure uses the past form of be and the past participle of the descriptive verb. The optional column below describes the person or people that are undertaking the action. Note, the subject (first column) is a noun phrase.

Positive Form	(Phrasal) Verb	Optional
The university	will be worked in	by me
The library	will be gone to	by you
The study room	will be studied in	by him
Her room	will be cried in	by her
Its kennel	will be slept in	by it
The park	will be run in	by (noun)
The snow	will be skied in	by us
The path	will be walked on	by them
Their subject	will be learned about	by (nouns)

Negative Form	(Phrasal) Verb	Optional
The party	is not being driven to	by me
The campus	is not being cycled across	by you
The heater	is not being dozed next to	by him
Her school	is not being eaten at	by her
His home	is not being barked near	by it
The salt	is not being reached for	by (noun)
The national park	is not being climbed in	by us
Their books	are not being looked at	by them
The shop	is not being served in	by (nouns)

Question Form	(Phrasal) Verb	Optional
Is your house	being eaten at	by me?
Is my house	being come past	by you?
Are the stairs	being walked up	by him?
Is her computer	being played on	by her?
Is a bone	being chewed on	by it?
Is a bridge	being walked under	by (noun)?
Is the party	being gone to	by us?
Is the aircraft	being flown away on	by them?
Are their iPads	being looked at	by (nouns)?

WITH TRANSITIVE VERBS

This verb structure uses a past tense version of **be**, that matches the subject, together with the past participle of the descriptive verb. The 'person' refers to who is the beneficiary/actor of the action. In the question form the preposition may need to be converted into an adjective for inclusion in the subject noun phrase in order to make sense (see the first person question form using 'had').

Noun Phrase	Verb	Preposition	Person
The newspaper	will be bought	at the local shop.	by me.
The reports	will be seen	from your boss.	by you.
Some noodles	will be eaten	at lunchtime.	by him.
Life insurance	will be sold	from her office.	by her.
The people	will be noticed	in the park.	by it.
The bus	will be ridden	to the office.	by (noun).
The same route	will be taken	in the morning.	by us.
Their evenings	will be spent	in the coffee shop.	by them.
The subjects	will be studied	in their books.	by (nouns)
Noun phrase	Verb	Preposition	Person
The crossword	will not be done	in the morning.	by me.
The answer	will not be known	to my question.	by you.
People	will not be brought	to the meeting.	by him.
Her own body	will not be loved	at the moment.	by her.
The food	will not be liked	in its bowl.	by it.
The students	will not be taught	on Friday.	by (noun).
French fries	will not be bought	at any time.	by us.
The bus	will not be caught	in the morning.	by them.
The meetings	will not be attended	in the office.	by (nouns).
Question	Verb	Preposition	Person
Will the class's attention	be had		by me?
Will a shower	be taken	in the mornings?	by you?
Will his notes	be written	during his class?	by him?
Will the cello	be played	in the orchestra?	by her?
Will holes	be dug	in the garden?	by it?
Will movies	be watched	after work?	by (noun)?
Will the party	be attended	at the club?	by us?
Will their car	be driven	on the footpath?	by them?
Will the posts	be found	on the website?	by (nouns)?

SIMPLE FUTURE PASSIVE

Positive Form		
	will be	by me.
	will be	by you.
	will be	by him.
	will be	by her.
	will be	by it.
	will be	by .
	will be	by us.
	will be	by them.
	will be	by

Negative Form		
	will not be	by me.
	will not be	by you.
	will not be	by him.
	will not be	by her.
	will not be	by it.
	will not be	by .
	will not be	by us.
	will not be	by them.
	will not be	by

Question Form		
Will	be	by me?
Will	be	by you?
Will	be	by him?
Will	be	by her?
Will	be	by it?
Will	be	by ?
Will	be	by us?
Will	be	by them?
Will	be	by ?

PRESENT CONTINUOUS PASSIVE

Creation: This tense is used to describe continuing actions being undertaken by or for someone or something else.

| **will** (modal) | **not** (optional) | **being** (aux) | **present participle** |

Examples: The dog **is being walked** (intransitive) *or* He **is being followed** home (transitive).

Note that the auxiliary verb **be** will match the object (**am** for 1st person singular; **are** for 2nd person singular and plural; **is** for 3rd person singular; and **are** for 1st and 3rd person plural) and will carry the tense's time period. The 2nd present participle auxiliary verb (**being**) carries the type of tense, signifying, in this case, that it is continuous.

Use this tense to describe the following:

Actions happening now undertaken by unknown persons: Use the present continuous to express the idea that something is ongoing now, at this very moment. It can also be used to show that something is not happening now.

Examples:

The car **is being driven** slowly

I **am not being asked** to give a speech.

Actions in progress that may not be imminently completed: used to describe being in the process of doing a longer action which is in progress; however, it might not be being done at this exact moment in time.

Examples: A survey **is being undertaken** *or* The report **is being studied.**

Imminent future actions by unknown persons: use to indicate that something has been planned to happen in the near future. Note that the emphasis is on the fact that the event was already planned prior to talking about it.

Examples:

The party **is being planned** for tonight

The play **is being performed** next week

Non habitual actions happening around now: use when the actions are happening around the present time and are not permanent.

Example: They **are being told** they can't leave their car here.

WITH INTRANSITIVE VERBS

Intransitive verbs are not used to create passive voice on their own but can be used in phrasal verbs. This structure uses the present form of **be**, the present participle of **be** and the past participle of the descriptive verb. The optional column below describes the person or people that are undertaking the action. Note, the subject (first column) is a noun phrase.

Positive Form	(Phrasal) Verb	Optional
The university	is being worked in	by me
The library	is being gone to	by you
The study room	is being studied in	by him
Her room	is being cried in	by her
Its kennel	is being slept in	by it
The park	is being run in	by (noun)
The snow	is being skied in	by us
The path	is being walked on	by them
Their subject	is being learned about	by (nouns)

Negative Form	(Phrasal) Verb	Optional
The party	is not being driven to	by me
The campus	is not being cycled across	by you
The heater	is not being dozed next to	by him
Her school	is not being eaten at	by her
His home	is not being barked near	by it
The salt	is not being reached for	by (noun)
The national park	is not being climbed in	by us
Their books	are not being looked at	by them
The shop	is not being served in	by (nouns)

Question Form	(Phrasal) Verb	Optional
Is your house	being eaten at	by me
Is my house	being come past	by you
Are the stairs	being walked up	by him
Is her computer	being played on	by her
Is a bone	being chewed on	by it
Is a bridge	being walked under	by (noun)
Is the party	being gone to	by us
Is the aircraft	being flown away on	by them
Are their iPads	being looked at	by (nouns)

Verb Tenses

WITH TRANSITIVE VERBS

This verb structure uses a present tense version of **be**, that matches the subject, the present participle of **be** and the past participle of the descriptive verb. The 'person' refers to who is the beneficiary/actor of the action. The example with the verb 'known' (shaded) is grammatically correct but very clumsy so it would usually be written using the simple tense as "The answer to my question is not known [by you]".

Noun Phrase	Verb	Preposition	Person
The newspaper	is being bought	at the local shop.	by me.
The reports	is being seen	from your boss.	by you.
Some noodles	are being eaten	at lunchtime.	by him.
Life insurance	is being sold	from her office.	by her.
The people	are being noticed	in the park.	by it.
The bus	is being ridden	to the office.	by (noun).
The same route	is being taken	in the morning.	by us.
Their evenings	are being spent	in the coffee shop.	by them.
The subjects	are being studied	in their books.	by (nouns)
Noun phrase	Verb	Preposition	Person
The crossword	is not being done	in the morning	by me.
The answer	is not being known	to my question	by you.
People	are not being brought	to the meeting	by him.
Her own body	is not being loved	at the moment	by her.
The food	is not being liked	in its bowl	by it.
The students	is not being taught	on Friday	by (noun).
French fries	are not being bought	at any time	by us.
The bus	is not being caught	in the morning	by them.
The meetings	are not being attended	in the office	by (nouns).
Question	Verb	Preposition	Person
Is the class's attention	being had		by me?
Is a shower	being taken	in the mornings?	by you?
Are his notes	being written	during his class?	by him?
Is the cello	being played	in the orchestra?	by her?
Are holes	being dug	in the garden?	by it?
Are movies	being watched	after work?	by (noun)?
Is the party	being attended	at the club?	by us?
Is their car	being driven	on the footpath?	by them?
Are the posts	being found	on the website?	by (nouns)?

PRESENT CONTINUOUS PASSIVE

Positive Form		
	being	by me.
	being	by you.
	being	by him.
	being	by her.
	being	by it.
	being	by .
	being	by us.
	being	by them.
	being	by

Negative Form		
	not being	by me.
	not being	by you.
	not being	by him.
	not being	by her.
	not being	by it.
	not being	by .
	not being	by us.
	not being	by them.
	not being	by

Question Form		
(Am/Is/Are)	being	by me?
(Am/Is/Are)	being	by you?
(Am/Is/Are)	being	by him?
(Am/Is/Are)	being	by her?
(Am/Is/Are)	being	by it?
(Am/Is/Are)	being	by ?
(Am/Is/Are)	being	by us?
(Am/Is/Are)	being	by them?
(Am/Is/Are)	being	by ?

PAST CONTINUOUS PASSIVE

Creation: This tense is used to describe continuing actions in the past that took place before another action in the past.

be (aux)	**not** (optional)	**being** (aux)	**past participle**

Note that the action being described was started before the particular moment but has not yet finished at that moment. In other words whenever this tense is used then it is usually based on the assumption that the listener knows what time is being talked about.

Use this tense to describe:

Interrupted action in the past undertaken by others: used to indicate that a longer action in the past was interrupted with an interruption of a shorter duration. It can be a real interruption or just an interruption in time. **Examples:**

The tests **were being conducted** when it broke. (unplanned interruption)
The horses **were being rested** for a couple of hours.   (timed interruption)

Specific time as an interruption to an event controlled by others: in addition to you can also use a specific time as an interruption. Note that the main difference between this tense and the simple past is that a specific time is used to show when an action began or finished whereas in this tense a specific time only interrupts the action, which continues after the delay. Note the use of the adverbs, <u>still</u> and <u>finally</u>, in the examples:

My damaged car **was** <u>still</u> **being fixed** at 6 p.m.
After an hour's delay, the flight **was** <u>finally</u> **being called**

Simultaneous actions by others: used to express the idea that two or more actions were happening at the same time and in parallel. The second action may (unknown actor) or may not (known actor) be passive. **Examples:**

She **was being taught** while I **played** on the computer (2nd not passive)
Some **were being bought** while others **were being sold** (both passive)

Atmosphere created by other people: it can also be used to describe a series of parallel actions to describe the atmosphere at a particular time in the past.

Example: Back then old people **were being cared for** and young people **were being taught** to respect others (**cared for** is a phrasal verb).

Annoyance at other people's action using always: This tense is often used to express annoyance at constantly repeated actions.

Example: We **were** always **being made** to look stupid by the boss.

WITH INTRANSITIVE VERBS

Intransitive verbs are not used to create passive voice on their own but can be used in phrasal verbs. This structure uses the past form of **be**, the present participle of **be** and the past participle of the descriptive verb. The optional column below describes the person or people that are undertaking the action. Note, the subject (first column) is a noun phrase.

Positive Form	(Phrasal) Verb	Optional
The university	was being worked in	by me
The library	was being gone to	by you
The study room	was being studied in	by him
Her room	was being cried in	by her
Its kennel	was being slept in	by it
The park	was being run in	by (noun)
The snow	was being skied in	by us
The path	was being walked on	by them
Their subject	was being learned about	by (nouns)
Negative Form	**(Phrasal) Verb**	**Optional**
The party	was not being driven to	by me
The campus	was not being cycled across	by you
The heater	was not being dozed next to	by him
Her school	was not being eaten at	by her
His home	was not being barked near	by it
The salt	was not being reached for	by (noun)
The national park	was not being climbed in	by us
Their books	were not being looked at	by them
The shop	was not being served in	by (nouns)
Question Form	**(Phrasal) Verb**	**Optional**
Was your house	being eaten at	by me
Was my house	being come past	by you
Were the stairs	being walked up	by him
Was her computer	being played on	by her
Was a bone	being chewed on	by it
Was a bridge	being walked under	by (noun)
Was the party	being gone to	by us
Was the aircraft	being flown away on	by them
Were their iPads	being looked at	by (nouns)

WITH TRANSITIVE VERBS

This verb structure uses a past tense version of **be**, that matches the subject, the present participle of **be** and the past participle of the descriptive verb. The 'person' refers to who is the beneficiary/actor of the action. The example with the verb 'known' (shaded) is grammatically correct but very clumsy so it would usually be written using the simple tense as "The answer to my question was not known [by you]".

Noun Phrase	Verb	Preposition	Person
The newspaper	was being bought	at the local shop.	by me.
The reports	was being seen	from your boss.	by you.
Some noodles	were being eaten	at lunchtime.	by him.
Life insurance	was being sold	from her office.	by her.
The people	were being noticed	in the park.	by it.
The bus	was being ridden	to the office.	by (noun).
The same route	was being taken	in the morning.	by us.
Their evenings	were being spent	in the coffee shop.	by them.
The subjects	were being studied	in their books.	by (nouns)
Noun phrase	Verb	Preposition	Person
The crossword	was not being done	in the morning	by me.
The answer	was not being known	to my question	by you.
People	were not being brought	to the meeting	by him.
Her own body	was not being loved	at the moment	by her.
The food	was not being liked	in its bowl	by it.
The students	was not being taught	on Friday	by (noun).
French fries	were not being bought	at any time	by us.
The bus	was not being caught	in the morning	by them.
The meetings	were not being attended	in the office	by (nouns).
Question	Verb	Preposition	Person
Was the class's attention	being had		by me?
Was a shower	being taken	in the mornings?	by you?
Were his notes	being written	during his class?	by him?
Was the cello	being played	in the orchestra?	by her?
Were holes	being dug	in the garden?	by it?
Were movies	being watched	after work?	by (noun)?
Was the party	being attended	at the club?	by us?
Was their car	being driven	on the footpath?	by them?
Were the posts	being found	on the website?	by (nouns)?

PAST CONTINUOUS PASSIVE

Positive Form		
	being	by me.
	being	by you.
	being	by him.
	being	by her.
	being	by it.
	being	by .
	being	by us.
	being	by them.
	being	by

Negative Form		
	not being	by me.
	not being	by you.
	not being	by him.
	not being	by her.
	not being	by it.
	not being	by .
	not being	by us.
	not being	by them.
	not being	by

Question Form		
(Was/Were)	being	by me?
(Was/Were)	being	by you?
(Was/Were)	being	by him?
(Was/Were)	being	by her?
(Was/Were)	being	by it?
(Was/Were)	being	by ?
(Was/Were)	being	by us?
(Was/Were)	being	by them?
(Was/Were)	being	by ?

FUTURE CONTINUOUS PASSIVE

Creation: This tense is used to describe continuing actions in the future that will take place before another action in the future.

will	not (option)	be	being	present participle

Examples: I **will not be being driven** by a driver today or She **will be being voted** in soon.

The modal verb, will, can be replaced to change the mood. **Examples:**

I **must** be being sent away soon. (Shows compulsion rather than intent)
I **might** be being promoted this year (Shows possibility rather than intent).

Use this tense to describe:

Future actions at a set time: use to say what will be happening at a fixed time in the future. Note, I know the person in the first example.

Example:

I **will be being played** at badminton at 6 p.m. (By an unnamed person).
I **will be being advised** this afternoon. (By an unknown person).

Interrupted action for somebody in the future: use this tense to indicate that a longer action in the future will be interrupted by a shorter action (usually expressed using an adverb clause) in the future.

Example: I **will be being massaged** when you arrive.

Specifying a timed interruption in the future: this tense can also be used to express an interruption that will happen at a <u>specific time</u>. **Examples:**

I **will be being stopped** from working by the power cut <u>this evening</u>.
She **will be being taken** to the supermarket <u>at 10 a.m.</u> to do her shopping.

Parallel actions in the future: you can also use this tense to describe two (or more) actions that are occurring simultaneously in the future. **Examples:**

I **will be being served** at a restaurant while my wife has to cook her dinner.
She **will be being checked** by her doctor while her husband is at work.

Predictions of social interaction in the future: this tense can be used to predict what sort of social interactions are likely to be happening at a future point in time, usually by describing parallel actions.

Example: The feeling is that we **will be being bored** by the lecture this afternoon, so I think many of my friends **will be being persuaded** to cut class and go to the mall instead.

WITH INTRANSITIVE VERBS

This structure uses a modal verb to denote the future, the present form of **be**, the present participle of **be** and the past participle of the descriptive verb in the form of a phrasal verb. The optional column below describes the person or people that are undertaking the action. Note, the subject (first column) is a noun phrase.

Positive Form	(Phrasal) Verb	Optional
The university	will be being worked in	by me
The library	will be being gone to	by you
The study room	will be being studied in	by him
Her room	will be being cried in	by her
Its kennel	will be being slept in	by it
The park	will be being run in	by (noun)
The snow	will be being skied in	by us
The path	will be being walked on	by them
Their subject	will be being learned about	by (nouns)
Negative Form	(Phrasal) Verb	Optional
The party	will not be being driven to	by me
The campus	will not be being cycled across	by you
The heater	will not be being dozed next to	by him
Her school	will not be being eaten at	by her
His home	will not be being barked near	by it
The salt	will not be being reached for	by (noun)
The national park	will not be being climbed in	by us
Their books	will not be being looked at	by them
The shop	will not be being served in	by (nouns)
Question Form	(Phrasal) Verb	Optional
Will your house	be being eaten at	by me
Will my house	be being come past	by you
Will the stairs	be being walked up	by him
Will her computer	be being played on	by her
Will a bone	be being chewed on	by it
Will a bridge	be being walked under	by (noun)
Will the party	be being gone to	by us
Will the aircraft	be being flown away on	by them
Will their iPads	be being looked at	by (nouns)

WITH TRANSITIVE VERBS

This verb structure uses a modal verb, the present tense version of **be**, the present participle of **be** and the past participle of the descriptive verb. Other types of modal verb can be used to change the intent or level of possibility. The person(s) are not shown for clarity, but they can be inferred from the page opposite.

Noun Phrase	Verb	Preposition
The newspaper	will be being bought	at the local shop
The reports	will be being seen	from your boss
Some noodles	will be being eaten	at lunchtime
Life insurance	will be being sold	from her office
The people	will be being noticed	in the park
The bus	will be being ridden	to the office
The same route	will be being taken	in the morning
Their evenings	will be being spent	in the coffee shop
The subjects	will be being studied	in their books
Noun phrase	Verb	Preposition
The crossword	will not be being done	in the morning
The answer	will not be being known	to my question
People	will not be being brought	to the meeting
Her own body	will not be being loved	at the moment
The food	will not be being liked	in its bowl
The students	will not be being taught	on Friday
French fries	will not be being bought	at any time
The bus	will not be being caught	in the morning
The meetings	will not be being attended	in the office
Question	Verb	Preposition
Will the class's attention	be being had	
Will a shower	be being taken	in the mornings?
Will his notes	be being written	during his class?
Will the cello	be being played	in the orchestra?
Will holes	be being dug	in the garden?
Will movies	be being watched	after work?
Will the party	be being attended	at the club?
Will their car	be being driven	on the footpath?
Will the posts	be being found	on the website?

FUTURE CONTINUOUS PASSIVE

Positive Form		
	will be being	by me.
	will be being	by you.
	will be being	by him.
	will be being	by her.
	will be being	by it.
	will be being	by .
	will be being	by us.
	will be being	by them.
	will be being	by

Negative Form		
	will not be being	by me.
	will not be being	by you.
	will not be being	by him.
	will not be being	by her.
	will not be being	by it.
	will not be being	by .
	will not be being	by us.
	will not be being	by them.
	will not be being	by

Question Form		
Will	be being	by me?
Will	be being	by you?
Will	be being	by him?
Will	be being	by her?
Will	be being	by it?
Will	be being	by ?
Will	be being	by us?
Will	be being	by them?
Will	be being	by ?

PRESENT PERFECT PASSIVE

Creation: This tense is used to describe a current action by someone or something with an emphasis on the result rather than when it happened.

have/has	not (if negative)	been (aux)	past participle

Examples: She has not been seen since Monday *or* **I have been left** alone.

Use this tense to describe the following:

Describe someone's experience: Use the present perfect to describe an experience undergone *or* that a certain experience has never been had, but **NOT** a specific event.

Example: She has been driven here *or* **I have not been interviewed** yet

Regrettable changes over a period of time: Use the Present Perfect to talk about change that has happened over a period of time.

Example: Many buildings **have been abandoned** over the past few years.

Highlight someone's accomplishments: Use the present perfect to list the accomplishments of people without giving a specific time.

Example: She **has been awarded** many prizes for her outstanding research.

Show dismay at something you were expecting to happen but didn't: use the present perfect to say that an action which was expected to happen but still hasn't happened.

Example: I don't know my score as the exams **have not been marked** yet.

Multiple actions by other people that have happened at different times: use the present perfect to talk about several different actions which have occurred in the past at different times. It can also be used to suggest that the process is not complete and more actions are possible.

Example: She **has been left** in charge, while the manager was on holiday.

Continuing situations by third parties: It can be used to indicate actions that have continued over a period of time.

Example: The war **has been fought** for a number of years

Expressing regret at a choice made by unknown people: It can be used to talk about things that cause a feeling of regret.

Example: Sadly, the work **has been curtailed** because of funding problems.

WITH INTRANSITIVE VERBS

This verb structure uses the present version of the verb **have** (have or has to match the subject), the past participle of **be** and the past participle of the descriptive verb. The prepositional phrases in the question form,s specify the time frames. The subject (first column) is a noun phrase.

Positive Form	(Phrasal) Verb	Optional
The university	has been worked in	by me
The library	has been gone to	by you
The study room	has been studied in	by him
Her room	has been cried in	by her
Its kennel	has been slept in	by it
The park	has been run in	by (noun)
The snow	has been skied in	by us
The path	has been walked on	by them
Their subject	has been learned about	by (nouns)
Negative Form	**(Phrasal) Verb**	**Optional**
The party	has not been driven to	by me
The campus	has not been cycled across	by you
The heater	has not been dozed next to	by him
Her school	has not been eaten at	by her
His home	has not been barked near	by it
The salt	has not been reached for	by (noun)
The national park	has not been climbed in	by us
Their books	has not been looked at	by them
The shop	has not been served in	by (nouns)
Question Form	**(Phrasal) Verb**	**Prepositional Phrase**
Has your house	been eaten at	in the evening?
Has my house	been come past	in the morning?
Have the stairs	been walked up	after his class?
Has her computer	been played on	at night?
Has a bone	been chewed on	in its kennel?
Has a bridge	been walked under	on his way home?
Has the party	been gone to	in the evening?
Has the aircraft	been flown away on	on the 17th?
Have their iPads	been looked at	under their desks?

WITH TRANSITIVE VERBS

This verb structure uses the present version of the verb **have** (have or has to match the subject), the past participle of **be** and the past participle of the descriptive verb. Additional prepositional phrases can be used after the verb. The example with the verb 'known' would usually be written using the simple tense as "The answer to my question is not known [by you]". The phrase 'at the moment' is not needed in the perfect tense.

Noun Phrase	Verb	Preposition	Person
The newspaper	has been bought	at the local shop.	by me.
The reports	has been seen	from your boss.	by you.
Some noodles	have been eaten	at lunchtime.	by him.
Life insurance	has been sold	from her office.	by her.
The people	has been noticed	in the park.	by it.
The bus	has been ridden	to the office.	by (noun).
The same route	has been taken	in the morning.	by us.
Their evenings	have been spent	in the coffee shop.	by them.
The subjects	have been studied	in their books.	by (nouns)

Noun phrase	Verb	Preposition	Person
The crossword	has not been done	in the morning	by me.
The answer	has not been known	to my question	by you.
People	have not been brought	to the meeting	by him.
Her own body	has not been loved	at the moment	by her.
The food	has not been liked	in its bowl	by it.
The students	has not been taught	on Friday	by (noun).
French fries	has not been bought	at any time	by us.
The bus	has not been caught	in the morning	by them.
The meetings	have not been attended	in the office	by (nouns).

Question	Verb	Preposition	Person
Has the class's attention	been had		by me?
Has a shower	been taken	in the mornings?	by you?
Have his notes	been written	during his class?	by him?
Has the cello	been played	in the orchestra?	by her?
Have holes	been dug	in the garden?	by it?
Have movies	been watched	after work?	by (noun)?
Has the party	been attended	at the club?	by us?
Has their car	been driven	on the footpath?	by them?
Have the posts	been found	on the website?	by (nouns)?

PRESENT PERFECT PASSIVE

Positive Form		
	been	by me.
	been	by you.
	been	by him.
	been	by her.
	been	by it.
	been	by .
	been	by us.
	been	by them.
	been	by .

Negative Form		
	not been	by me.
	not been	by you.
	not been	by him.
	not been	by her.
	not been	by it.
	not been	by .
	not been	by us.
	not been	by them.
	not been	by .

Question Form		
(Has/Have)	been	by me?
(Has/Have)	been	by you?
(Has/Have)	been	by him?
(Has/Have)	been	by her?
(Has/Have)	been	by it?
(Has/Have)	been	by ?
(Has/Have)	been	by us?
(Has/Have)	been	by them?
(Has/Have)	been	by ?

PAST PERFECT PASSIVE

Creation: This tense is used to describe an action in the past that took place before another action in the past. It takes the form:

had (aux)	**not** (if negative)	**been** (aux)	**past participle**

Examples: He **had not been contacted** as promised *or* The mine **had been worked** as recently as two years ago, but is now closed.

Use this tense to describe:

Conditionals or to justify conclusions: see opposite page.

Reported speech: Past perfect is often used in reported speech after the verbs <u>asked</u>, <u>explained</u>, <u>said</u>, <u>told</u>, <u>thought</u> *or* <u>wondered</u> had already been used in the sentence. For example study the following paragraph:

The company's manager <u>**explained**</u> why the redundancies **had been sent** out. He <u>**said**</u> the company **had been hit** by a downturn in the market. The workers <u>**told**</u> him that they **had been shocked** to be suddenly terminated. The manager <u>**thought**</u> that they **had** already **been informed**, by letter, weeks before. The workers <u>**wondered**</u> if they **had been told** the truth by the management. A newspaper reporter then <u>**asked**</u> what **had been done** to improve morale at the firm after the shock news.

Action completed by others before another action in the past: used to show that something happened before a specific time or action in the past. The times can be expressed either in relative or absolute terms. **Examples:**

The rubbish **had not been removed** since last month (relative time)
The bag **had not been moved** for the last two hours (absolute time)

Specific timed events: this tense can be used, unlike Present Perfect, to express a specific time. But it is optional in that if the words <u>before</u> or <u>after</u> are used in the sentence then it becomes simple past. The first example sentence uses past perfect whereas the second uses simple past.

York Minster **had been built** in 627 but **had been burned** down in 741
Gothic **was** popular <u>after</u> the Norman Conquest and <u>before</u> the reformation

Lack of something: This tense can be used to express a lack of something rather than an action.

Examples: None of the invitations **had been received** by anyone on the list

Reason for a past action by others: use for supplying a reason for course of action undertaken in the past. **Example:**

Her arrival was a surprise as she **had not been expected** to attend.

WITH INTRANSITIVE VERBS

This verb structure is commonly used to express conditionals. For example the statement forms could be prefaced with 'if' and suffixed with 'then' and used to express a, now impossible, outcome. Without the 'if' it would be used to provide a conclusion with 'so'. The question form shows what would be true if something different had happened.

Positive Form	(Phrasal) Verb	Outcome
If the university	had been worked in	then… / so…
If the library	had been gone to	then… / so…
If the study room	had been studied in	then… / so…
If her room	had been cried in	then… / so…
If its kennel	had been slept in	then… / so…
If the park	had been run in	then… / so…
If the snow	had been skied in	then… / so…
If the path	had been walked on	then… / so…
If their subject	had been learned about	then… / so…

Negative Form	(Phrasal) Verb	Outcome
If the party	had not been driven to	then… / so…
If the campus	had not been cycled across	then… / so…
If the heater	had not been dozed next to	then… / so…
If her school	had not been eaten at	then… / so…
If his home	had not been barked near	then… / so…
If the salt	had not been reached for	then… / so…
If the national park	had not been climbed in	then… / so…
If their books	had not been looked at	then… / so…
If the shop	had not been served in	then… / so…

Question Form	(Phrasal) Verb	Outcome
Had your house	been eaten at	then…
Had my house	been come past	then…
Had the stairs	been walked up	then…
Had her computer	been played on	then…
Had a bone	been chewed on	then…
Had a bridge	been walked under	then…
Had the party	been gone to	then…
Had their holiday	been flown away on	then…
Had their iPads	been looked at	then…

Verb Tenses

WITH TRANSITIVE VERBS

This verb structure is commonly used to express conditionals. For example the statement forms could be prefaced with 'if' and suffixed with 'then' and used to express a, now impossible, outcome. Without the 'if' it would be used to provide a conclusion with 'so'. The question form shows what would be true if something different had happened. The phrase at the moment is not used in this tense - use at **that** moment instead.

Noun Phrase	Verb	Preposition	Outcome
The newspaper	had been bought	at the local shop.	so...
The reports	had been seen	from your boss.	so...
Some noodles	had been eaten	at lunchtime.	so...
Life insurance	had been sold	from her office.	so...
The people	had been noticed	in the park.	so...
The bus	had been ridden	to the office.	so...
The same route	had been taken	in the morning.	so...
Their evenings	had been spent	in the coffee shop.	so...
The subjects	had been studied	in their books.	so...
Noun phrase	Verb	Preposition	Outcome
The crossword	had not been done	in the morning	so...
The answer	had not been known	to my question	so...
People	had not been brought	to the meeting	so...
Her own body	had not been loved	at the moment	so...
The food	has not been liked	in its bowl	so...
The students	had not been taught	on Friday	so...
French fries	had not been bought	at any time	so...
The bus	had not been caught	in the morning	so...
The meetings	had not been attended	in the office	so...
Question	Verb	Preposition	Outcome
Had the class's attention	been had		then...
Had a shower	been taken	in the mornings?	then...
Had his notes	been written	during his class?	then...
Had the cello	been played	in the orchestra?	then...
Had holes	been dug	in the garden?	then...
Had movies	been watched	after work?	then...
Had the party	been attended	at the club?	then...
Had their car	been driven	on the footpath?	then...
Had the posts	been found	on the website?	then...

PRESENT PERFECT PASSIVE

Positive Form	
had been	
had been	
had been	
had been	
had been	
had been	
had been	
had been	
had been	

Negative Form	
had not been	
had not been	
had not been	
had not been	
had not been	
had not been	
had not been	
had not been	
had not been	

Question Form		
Had	been	then
Had	been	then
Had	been	then
Had	been	then
Had	been	then
Had	been	then
Had	been	then
Had	been	then
Had	been	then

FUTURE PERFECT PASSIVE

Creation: This tense is used to describe an action in the future that will take place before another action in the future. It takes the form:

| will | not (option) | have | been | past participle |

Examples: I **will not have been informed** by her *or* She **will have been taken** to see her new house by this afternoon.

Other (true) modal verbs can be used with this tense to express different intent or feelings.

Examples:

You **will have been informed** about the results by noon. *definite action*
You **have to have been given** permission to enter. *action by others needed*
It **must have been lost** when I moved. *providing a logical explanation*
You **need to have been passed** by the teacher first. *stating a requirement*
We **shall have been fed** by the time you arrive. *prediction of an event*
Can you **have been misled** by the false data? *stating a possibility*
I **ought to have been promoted** by now. *action that should have happened*
You **should have been taught** it at school. *best action that didn't happen*
I **would have been sent** but they sent her instead. *reason for inaction*
The car **may have been damaged** in the flood. *give a possible explanation*
It **might have just been** a coincidence. *expressing an unlikely possibility*
I **could have been told** that at the time. *an action that would have helped*

Use this tense to describe:

Completed action by someone before a time in the future: use this tense to describe an action that will happen before a time in the future

She **will have been transformed** into a super-model by next year
He will be late home because he **will have been made** to finish his work

Completed action before another action in the future: use this tense to describe an action that will happen before another action in the future.

Example: We **need to have been told** about it before we can start.

Action that affects a future action: Describes past action that has taken place that happens before or within the timescale of another action.

I **will have been given** a car to use when I go on the trip. (Before)
During our holiday we **will have been taken** all around Asia. (Within)

WITH INTRANSITIVE VERBS

This verb structure uses a modal verb, the present version of the verb **have**, the past participle of **be** and the past participle of the descriptive verb. The prepositional phrases in the question form specify the time frames. The subject (first column) is a noun phrase.

Positive Form	(Phrasal) Verb	Optional
The university	will have been worked in	by me
The library	will have been gone to	by you
The study room	will have been studied in	by him
Her room	will have been cried in	by her
Its kennel	will have been slept in	by it
The park	will have been run in	by (noun)
The snow	will have been skied in	by us
The path	will have been walked on	by them
Their subject	will have been learned about	by (nouns)

Negative Form	(Phrasal) Verb	Optional
The party	will not have been driven to	by me
The campus	will not have been cycled across	by you
The heater	will not have been dozed next to	by him
Her school	will not have been eaten at	by her
His home	will not have been barked near	by it
The salt	will not have been reached for	by (noun)
The national park	will not have been climbed in	by us
Their books	will not have been looked at	by them
The shop	will not have been served in	by (nouns)

Question Form	(Phrasal) Verb	Prepositional Phrase
Will your house	have been eaten at	in the evening?
Will my house	have been come past	in the morning?
Will the stairs	have been walked up	after his class?
Will her computer	have been played on	at night?
Will a bone	have been chewed on	in its kennel?
Will a bridge	have been walked under	on his way home?
Will the party	have been gone to	in the evening?
Will the aircraft	have been flown away on	on the 17th?
Will their iPads	have been looked at	under their desks?

WITH TRANSITIVE VERBS

This verb structure uses a modal verb, the present version of the verb **have**, the past participle of **be** and the past participle of the descriptive verb. The prepositional phrases that were used in previous tenses have been omitted for clarity; however, they can be used after the verb. The example using known would not have a prepositional phrase inserted after the verb, it would be inserted before the verb instead.

Noun Phrase	Verb	Person
The newspaper	will have been bought	by me.
The reports	will have been seen	by you.
Some noodles	will have been eaten	by him.
Life insurance	will have been sold	by her.
The people	will have been noticed	by it.
The bus	will have been ridden	by (noun).
The same route	will have been taken	by us.
Their evenings	will have been spent	by them.
The subjects	will have been studied	by (nouns)
Noun phrase	Verb	Person
The crossword	will not have been done	by me.
The answer	will not have been known	by you.
People	will not have been brought	by him.
Her own body	will not have been loved	by her.
The food	will not have been liked	by it.
The students	will not have been taught	by (noun).
French fries	will not have been bought	by us.
The bus	will not have been caught	by them.
The meetings	will not have been attended	by (nouns).
Question	Verb	Person
Will the class's attention	have been had	by me?
Will a shower	have been taken	by you?
Will his notes	have been written	by him?
Will the cello	have been played	by her?
Will holes	have been dug	by it?
Will movies	have been watched	by (noun)?
Will the party	have been attended	by us?
Will their car	have been driven	by them?
Will the posts	have been found	by (nouns)?

FUTURE PERFECT PASSIVE

Positive Form		
will have been		by me.
will have been		by you.
will have been		by him.
will have been		by her.
will have been		by it.
will have been		by .
will have been		by us.
will have been		by them.
will have been		by .

Negative Form		
will not have been		by me.
will not have been		by you.
will not have been		by him.
will not have been		by her.
will not have been		by it.
will not have been		by .
will not have been		by us.
will not have been		by them.
will not have been		by .

Question Form		
Will	have been	by me?
Will	have been	by you?
Will	have been	by him?
Will	have been	by her?
Will	have been	by it?
Will	have been	by ?
Will	have been	by us?
Will	have been	by them?
Will	have been	by ?

Verb Tenses

PRESENT PERFECT CONTINUOUS

Creation: This tense is used to describe continuing actions happening now in terms of their duration.

has/have	not (optional)	been	being (aux)	present participle

Examples: You **have not been being downgraded** since I took over as your boss

This is not a commonly used passive verb structure primarily because it appears difficult to use and because it is limited in what it can be used for. The duration is indicated by the use of '**for**' (to say how long something happened for) or '**since**' (signifying the start point for the continuing action). Note that **for** may be used with any tense, whereas **since** is tends to be used only with perfect tenses.

Examples:
The house **has been being renovated <u>for</u>** five years
Her car **has been being fixed <u>since</u>** last week

Use this tense to describe the following:

Gradual process undertaken from the past until now: use to show that something started in the past and has continued, usually in a methodical or controlled way, up until now. Any time duration from the past can be used right up until this very instant.

Example:
The lecture **has been being given** since noon
I **have been being brought** cups of tea all afternoon.

Actions recently completed: Used without the duration the tense has a more general meaning of something happening lately. You can use the adverbs <u>lately</u> or <u>recently</u> to emphasize this meaning.

Examples:
What **has been being resolved** <u>lately</u>
Has the work **been being checked** <u>recently</u>?

Defining a cause that is the fault of others: This tense can be used with adverbial clauses to describe why something happened, using a coordinating conjunction such as <u>because</u> or <u>as</u>. **Examples:**

The bus **has not been being used** <u>because</u> its brakes have failed.
The grades **have not been being given out** <u>as</u> the teacher is ill.

WITH INTRANSITIVE VERBS

This verb structure uses the present version of the verb **have** (have or has to match the subject), the past participle of **be** and the past participle of the descriptive verb. The prepositional phrases express the duration, extra prepositional phrases can be added afterwards to show context.

Positive Form	(Phrasal) Verb	Duration
The university	has been being worked in	for 2 years
The library	has been being gone to	for months
The study room	has been being studied in	for 8 hours
Her room	has been being cried in	every day for…
Its kennel	has been being slept in	for 12 hours
The park	has been being run in	since noon
The snow	has been being skied in	all day
The path	has been being walked on	for 3 days
Their subject	has been being learned about	for 8 hours

Negative Form	(Phrasal) Verb	Duration
The party	has not been being driven to	for a week
The campus	has not been being cycled across	for a month
The heater	has not been being dozed next to	for 2 hours
Her school	has not been being eaten at	for weeks
His home	has not been being barked near	for hours
The salt	has not been being reached for	for ten days
The national park	has not been being climbed in	for five years
Their books	has not been being looked at	for 2 weeks
The shop	has not been being served in	for 3 weeks

Question Form	(Phrasal) Verb	Duration
Has your house	been being eaten at	for 2 hours
Has my house	been being come past	for 3 hours
Have the stairs	been being walked up	for days
Has her computer	been being played on	for hours
Has a bone	been being chewed on	since the morning
Has a bridge	been being walked under	for hours
Has the party	been being gone to	for ages
Has the aircraft	been being flown away on	for hours
Have their iPads	been being looked at	for ten hours

WITH TRANSITIVE VERBS

This verb structure uses the present version of the verb **have** (have or has to match the subject), the past participle of **be, the present participle of be** and the past participle of the descriptive verb. The prepositional phrases after the verb have been changed to express the duration. Extra prepositional phrases can be added after the duration and a noun phrase can be added after the verb.

Noun Phrase	Verb	Duration
The newspaper	has been being bought	for 2 years
The reports	has been being seen	for months
Some noodles	have been being eaten	for 8 hours
Life insurance	has been being sold	every day
The people	has been being noticed	for 12 hours
The bus	has been being ridden	since noon
The same route	has been being taken	all day
Their evenings	have been being spent	for 3 days
The subjects	have been being studied	for 8 hours
Noun phrase	Verb	Duration
The crossword	has not been being done	for a week
The answer	has not been being known	for a month
People	have not been being brought	for 2 hours
Her own body	has not been being loved	for weeks
The food	has not been being liked	for hours
The students	has not been being taught	for ten days
French fries	has not been being bought	for five years
The bus	has not been being caught	for 2 weeks
The meetings	have not been being attended	for 3 weeks
Question	Verb	Duration
Has the class's attention	been being had	for 2 hours
Has a shower	been being taken	for 3 hours
Have his notes	been being written	for days
Has the cello	been being played	for hours
Have holes	been being dug	since the morning
Have movies	been being watched	for hours
Has the party	been being attended	for ages
Has their car	been being driven	for hours
Have the posts	been being found	for ten hours

PRESENT PERFECT PASSIVE

	Positive Form	
	been being	
	been being	
	been being	
	been being	
	been being	
	been being	
	been being	
	been being	
	been being	
	Negative Form	
	not been being	
	not been being	
	not been being	
	not been being	
	not been being	
	not been being	
	not been being	
	not been being	
	not been being	
	Question Form	
(Has/Have)	been being	
(Has/Have)	been being	
(Has/Have)	been being	
(Has/Have)	been being	
(Has/Have)	been being	
(Has/Have)	been being	
(Has/Have)	been being	
(Has/Have)	been being	
(Has/Have)	been being	

Verb Tenses

PAST PERFECT CONTINUOUS

Creation: This tense is used to describe continuing actions in the past by someone that took place before another action in the past.

had	not (optional)	been	being	past participle

Examples: The drinks **had been being created** by an expert or She **had not been being trusted** by anyone while she was here

Note that this tense differs from past perfect in that the action is over a longer time period. This tense is seldom used.

Use this tense to describe:

Duration of something before something in the past: use this tense to describe the duration of an action in the past that was interrupted or finished by a subsequent action. Note the question form.

Example: How long **had** you **been being kept** standing around before they picked you up?

Cause of something in the past: this tense can be used to show both the cause and the effect of something.

Examples: The army's reputation **had been being tarnished** by their inaction.

Effect of something in the past: this tense can also be used to state the effect of something based on a previous incident.

Example: The system broke down because it **had been being operated** without any maintenance.

Past Perfect Continuous versus Present Perfect Continuous

At first glance the two tenses are almost identical in both construction and meaning. The difference being that in past perfect continuous the action has already taken place and has already finished in the past; whereas with present perfect continuous the action is either still happening or has only just finished. Consider the following sentences:

I was weak as **I had been being operated** on for eight hours. (Past Perfect Continuous – I am not feeling weak now)

I am weak as **I have been being operated** on for eight hours. (Present Perfect Continuous – I am feeling weak at this time)

The first sentence gave a reason for a past event (I <u>was</u> weak); the second gives a reason for a current event (I <u>am</u> weak).

WITH INTRANSITIVE VERBS

This verb structure uses the past version of the verb **have**, the past participle of **be** and the past participle of the descriptive verb. The prepositional phrases express the duration. The question form is commonly used to state the effect of a past continuous action.

Positive Form	(Phrasal) Verb	Duration
The university	had been being worked in	for 2 years
The library	had been being gone to	for months
The study room	had been being studied in	for 8 hours
Her room	had been being cried in	every day
Its kennel	had been being slept in	for 12 hours
The park	had been being run in	since noon
The snow	had been being skied in	all day
The path	had been being walked on	for 3 days
Their subject	had been being learned about	for 8 hours

Negative Form	(Phrasal) Verb	Duration
The party	had not been being driven to	for a week
The campus	had not been being cycled across	for a month
The heater	had not been being dozed next to	for 2 hours
Her school	had not been being eaten at	for weeks
His home	had not been being barked near	for hours
The salt	had not been being reached for	for ten days
The national park	had not been being climbed in	for five years
Their books	had not been being looked at	for 2 weeks
The shop	had not been being served in	for 3 weeks

Question Form	(Phrasal) Verb	Effect
Had your house	been being eaten at	then...
Had my house	been being come past	then...
Had the stairs	been being walked up	then...
Had her computer	been being played on	then...
Had a bone	been being chewed on	then...
Had a bridge	been being walked under	then...
Had the party	been being gone to	then...
Had the aircraft	been being flown away on	then...
Had their iPads	been being looked at	then...

WITH TRANSITIVE VERBS

This verb structure uses the past version of the verb **have**, the past participle of **be** and the past participle of the descriptive verb. The prepositional phrases express the duration. The question form is commonly used to state the effect of a past continuous action. Extra prepositional phrases can be added after the duration and a noun phrase can be added after the verb.

Noun Phrase	Verb	Duration
The newspaper	had been being bought	for 2 years
The reports	had been being seen	for months
Some noodles	had been being eaten	for 8 hours
Life insurance	had been being sold	every day for…
The people	had been being noticed	for 12 hours
The bus	had been being ridden	since noon
The same route	had been being taken	all day
Their evenings	had been being spent	for 3 days
The subjects	had been being studied	for 8 hours
Noun phrase	Verb	Duration
The crossword	had not been being done	for a week
The answer	had not been being known	for a month
People	had not been being brought	for 2 hours
Her own body	had not been being loved	for weeks
The food	had not been being liked	for hours
The students	had not been being taught	for ten days
French fries	had not been being bought	for five years
The bus	had not been being caught	for 2 weeks
The meetings	had not been being attended	for 3 weeks
Question	Verb	Effect
Had the class's attention	been being had	then…
Had a shower	been being taken	then…
Had his notes	been being written	then…
Had the cello	been being played	then…
Had holes	been being dug	then…
Had movies	been being watched	then…
Had the party	been being attended	then…
Had their car	been being driven	then…
Had the posts	been being found	then…

PAST PERFECT PASSIVE

Positive Form		
had	been being	
had	been being	
had	been being	
had	been being	
had	been being	
had	been being	
had	been being	
had	been being	
had	been being	

Negative Form		
had	not been being	
had	not been being	
had	not been being	
had	not been being	
had	not been being	
had	not been being	
had	not been being	
had	not been being	
had	not been being	

Question Form		
Had	been being	then
Had	been being	then
Had	been being	then
Had	been being	then
Had	been being	then
Had	been being	then
Had	been being	then
Had	been being	then
Had	been being	then

Verb Tenses

FUTURE PERFECT CONTINUOUS

Creation: This tense is used to describe continuing actions in the future that will take place before another action in the future.

will	not (option)	have	been	being	present participle

Examples: She **will not have been being called** today *or* I **will have been being serenaded** for ten hours by tonight.

This is not a commonly used tense as it is perceived as being difficult to use and its uses are limited.

Use this tense to describe:

Duration of an action before another action in the future: Use to describe something that will happen up to or until another event or action in the future. It is like both the present perfect continuous and the past perfect continuous but, unlike them, it stops at a set point in the future. Note the duration in the examples:

I'll have been being made to wait at the airport all day for her.

He'll have been being employed here for 30 years by the time he retires.

Cause or effect of something in the future: can also be used (together with the word **because**) to show cause and effect of an event or action at a predetermined point in the future.

Examples:

She **will have been being stranded** for ages because I forgot to meet her.

He **will have been being bored** for hours because his television is broken.

Future Continuous versus Future Perfect Continuous

While the two tenses may look similar they have different meanings. Future continuous emphasizes a particular point in time, whereas future perfect continuous emphasizes the duration of an action (which may occur more than once). Consider the examples below to understand the difference:

First the future continuous:

I **will be being awoken** at 8 p.m.   At that point in time I will be woken up

Now the future perfect continuous:

I **will have been being awoken** since 6 p.m. Someone or something has been continuously or repetitively waking me up from 6 p.m. until now.

Two further examples show how the duration is highlighted in future perfect continuous: The first example is future continuous and the second is future perfect continuous. Note the timescale in the second example.

I **will be being entertained** when you arrive.

I **will have been being entertained** for two hours when you arrive.

WITH INTRANSITIVE VERBS

This verb structure uses a **modal**, the present version of the verb **have**, the past participle of **be**, the present participle of **be** and the past participle of the descriptive verb. The first preposition points to the duration and the second points to the end point. Pronouns have been used as subjects for clarity. The verb **eaten** has been changed to **fed** for obvious reasons.

Positive	(Phrasal) Verb	Duration	End
I	will have been being worked in	for/since	at/by
You	will have been being gone to	for/since	at/by
He	will have been being studied in	for/since	at/by
She	will have been being cried in	for/since	at/by
It	will have been being slept in	for/since	at/by
(Noun)	will have been being run in	for/since	at/by
We	will have been being skied in	for/since	at/by
They	will have been being walked on	for/since	at/by
(Nouns)	will have been being learned about	for/since	at/by
Negative	**(Phrasal) Verb**	**Duration**	**End**
I	will have not been being driven to	for/since	at/by
You	will have not been being cycled across	for/since	at/by
He	will have not been being dozed next to	for/since	at/by
She	will have not been being fed with...	for/since	at/by
It	will have not been being barked near	for/since	at/by
(Noun)	will have not been being reached for	for/since	at/by
We	will have not been being climbed in	for/since	at/by
They	will have not been being looked at	for/since	at/by
(Nouns)	will have not been being served in	for/since	at/by
Question	**(Phrasal) Verb**	**Duration**	**End**
Will I	have been being fed at...	for/since	at/by
Will you	have been being come past	for/since	at/by
Will he	have been being walked up	for/since	at/by
Will she	have been being played on	for/since	at/by
Will it	have been being chewed on	for/since	at/by
Will (noun)	have been being walked under	for/since	at/by
Will we	have been being gone to	for/since	at/by
Will they	have been being flown away on	for/since	at/by
Will (nouns)	have been being looked at	for/since	at/by

WITH TRANSITIVE VERBS

This verb structure uses a **modal**, the present version of the verb **have**, the past participle of **be,** the present participle of **be** and the past participle of the descriptive verb. The first preposition points to the duration and the second points to the end point. Pronouns have been used as subjects for clarity. Extra prepositional phrases can be added after the verb and/or the end and a noun phrase can be added after the verb.

Positive	Verb	Duration	End
I	will have been being bought	for/since	at/by
You	will have been being seen	for/since	at/by
He	will have been being fed	for/since	at/by
She	will have been being noticed	for/since	at/by
It	will have been being sold	for/since	at/by
(Noun)	will have been being ridden	for/since	at/by
We	will have been being taken	for/since	at/by
They	will have been being spent	for/since	at/by
(Nouns)	will have been being studied	for/since	at/by
Negative	**Verb**	**Duration**	**End**
I	will have not been being done	for/since	at/by
You	will have not been being known	for/since	at/by
He	will have not been being brought	for/since	at/by
She	will have not been being loved	for/since	at/by
It	will have not been being liked	for/since	at/by
(Noun)	will have not been being taught	for/since	at/by
We	will have not been being carried	for/since	at/by
They	will have not been being caught	for/since	at/by
(Nouns)	will have not been being attended	for/since	at/by
Question	**Verb**	**Duration**	**End**
Will I	have been being taken	for/since	at/by
Will you	have been being written about	for/since	at/by
Will he	have been being played	for/since	at/by
Will she	have been being watched	for/since	at/by
Will it	have been being dug	for/since	at/by
Will (noun)	have been being attended	for/since	at/by
Will we	have been being driven	for/since	at/by
Will they	have been being found	for/since	at/by
Will (nouns)	have been being seen	for/since	at/by

FUTURE PERFECT CONTINUOUS

Positive			
Sarah	**will have been being** taught	for 2 hrs	at 11
	will have been being		
	will have been being		
	will have been being		
	will have been being		
	will have been being		
	will have been being		
	will have been being		
	will have been being		

Negative			
	will have not been being		
	will have not been being		
	will have not been being		
	will have not been being		
	will have not been being		
	will have not been being		
	will have not been being		
	will have not been being		
	will have not been being		

Question		
Will	have been being	
Will	have been being	
Will	have been being	
Will	have been being	
Will	have been being	
Will	have been being	
Will	have been being	
Will	have been being	
Will	have been being	

TENSE SELECTOR

In this section you will find links to how the various tense structures and components are used in English.

Simply choose what you want to say and follow the link to a full explanation of how it works; plus, examples of it being used.

TENSE SELECTOR

TENSE SELECTOR

D

TENSE SELECTOR

Tense Selector

TENSE SELECTOR

TENSE SELECTOR

TENSE SELECTOR

E

TENSE SELECTOR

TENSE SELECTOR

F

TENSE SELECTOR

G

Tense Selector

TENSE SELECTOR

TENSE SELECTOR

TENSE SELECTOR

TENSE SELECTOR

M

TENSE SELECTOR

TENSE SELECTOR

R

TENSE SELECTOR

S

TENSE SELECTOR

TENSE SELECTOR

TENSE SELECTOR

T

TENSE SELECTOR

TENSE SELECTOR

TENSE SELECTOR

TENSE SELECTOR

TENSE SELECTOR

V

ENGLISHBOOK.SHOP

Where you come to learn

The free companion website provides a number of useful tools. One of the most useful tools when working with verbs is the custom search facility. This tool, shown below, allows you to type in a verb structure, together with other keywords, and it then searches a number of high quality, international publications and newspapers to match your criteria. In the example below the verb structure "have been used" (note the "speech marks") together with the keyword "computers".

Phrase Search - enter a phrase in "commas" to see it in use

"have been used" + "computers"

Clicking the search button opened a pop up window on which the first entry was:

Are programs better than people at predicting reoffending

https www economist com are-programs-better-than-people-at-predicting-reoffending

 Jan 17, 2018 ... IN AMERICA, computers have been used to assist bail and

Clicking on the link brought up the full article so the reference can be seen in the context in which it is used. The resulting paragraph looked like this:

IN AMERICA, computers have been used to assist bail and sentencing decisions for many years. Their proponents argue that the rigorous logic of an algorithm, trained with a vast amount of data, can make judgments about whether a convict will reoffend that are unclouded by human bias.

Source: The Economist - The full article can be found at:
https://www.economist.com/science-and-technology/2018/01/17/are-programs-better-than-people-at-predicting-reoffending

Using this tool and the dictionary on the site, you can search for any combination of tense structures and keywords to give you ideas on how you can structure your own sentences based on the results and the CORE colours. The website can be reached by using the QR code or the URL on the bottom of the page.

www.englishbook.shop